INSTANT
pressure cooker meals

Cook-At-Home Everyday Easy & Healthy Recipes, Delicious Pressure Cooker Meals

---

JULIA MOORE

Copyright Legal Information

© Copyright 2016 - All rights reserved.

In no way is it legal to reproduce, duplicate, or transmit any part of this document in either electronic means or in printed format. Recording of this publication is strictly prohibited and any storage of this document is not allowed unless with written permission from the publisher. All rights reserved.

The information provided herein is stated to be truthful and consistent, in that any liability, in terms of inattention or otherwise, by any usage or abuse of any policies, processes, or directions contained within is the solitary and utter responsibility of the recipient reader. Under no circumstances will any legal responsibility or blame be held against the publisher for any reparation, damages, or monetary loss due to the information herein, either directly or indirectly. Respective authors own all copyrights not held by the publisher.

Legal Notice:

This book is copyright protected. This is only for personal use. You cannot amend, distribute, sell, use, quote or paraphrase any part or the content within this book without the consent of the author or copyright owner. Legal action will be pursued if this is breached.

Disclaimer Notice:

Please note the information contained within this document is for educational and entertainment purposes only. Every attempt has been made to provide accurate, up to date and reliable complete information. No warranties of any kind are expressed or implied. Readers acknowledge that the author is not engaging in the rendering of legal, financial, medical or professional advice.

By reading this document, the reader agrees that under no circumstances are we responsible for any losses, direct or indirect, which are incurred as a result of the use of information contained within this document, including, but not limited to, —errors, omissions, or inaccuracies.

Table of Contents

Copyright Legal Information 2

Introduction 8

Three Generations of Electric Pressure Cookers 12

Reasons for Buying the Pressure Cooker 14

Pressure Release Guide and Terminology 18

How to Use the Pressure Cooker 19

The control Panel on an Pressure Cooker 21

Safety Features 26

Conversion Chart 30

Pressure Cooker Breakfast Recipes 34

Lemon Blueberry Steel Cut Oats 35

Oatmeal Apple Crisp 36

Chocolate Chip French toast 37

Creamy Cheesy Grits 38

Breakfast Burrito 39

Cheesy Egg Bake 40

Vegan Quiche 41

No Crust Quiche 42

Mexican Breakfast Casserole 43

Breakfast Hash 44

Pressure Cooker Sauce Recipes 45

HOW TO MIX YOUR OWN SEASONING 46

Fresh Tomato Sauce 47

Ragu (Meat Sauce) 48

Italian Spaghetti Meat Sauce 49

Ball Game Hot Dog Sauce 50

Mediterranean Eggplant Sauce 51

Tomato Basil Sauce 52

Marinara Sauce 53

Pressure Cooker Pizza Sauce 54

Pressure Cooker Bolognese Sauce 55

Pressure Cooker Soups Stews Recipes 56

Cream of Chicken Mushroom Soup 57

Chicken Vegetable Soup 59

Spanish Sardines and Tomato Soup 60

Creamy Crab Soup 61

Vegetable Hamburger Soup 62

Hearty Beef Quinoa Soup 63

Hearty Beef Cabbage Soup 64

Broccoli Cheddar Cheese Soup 65

Rustic Vegetable Soup 66

Creamy Pumpkin Corn Soup 67

Cream of Zucchini Soup 69

Winter Vegetable Soup 70

Meatball and Vegetable Soup 72

Lemon Garlic Lamb Stew 74

German Style Sausage Stew 76

Pressure Cooker Seafood Chowder 77

Easy Sunday Chili 79

Easy Sunday Vegan Chili 80

Pressure Cooker Appetizers Recipes 81

BBQ Sauce Chicken Drumsticks 82

Honey Teriyaki Chicken Wings 83

Pressure Cooker Chicken Paprika 84

Sweet and Spicy Meatballs 85

Barbecue Pork Ribs 86

BBQ Smoked Sausage 87

Chinese Boiled Peanuts 88

Sweet and Sour Meatballs 89

Corn on the Cob 90

The Ultimate Loaded Potato Skins 91

Eggplant Caponatina 93

- Crispy Roasted Yukon Potatoes 94
- Easy Hummus Dip 95
- Thai Baked Sweet Potatoes 95
- Ginger Honey Glazed Carrots 97
- Garlic Mashed Potatoes 98
- Wild Mushroom Risotto 99
- Root Vegetable Medley 100
- **Pressure Cooker Meat Poultry Recipes** 101
- Spicy Honey Garlic Chicken 102
- Pressure Cooker Roast Chicken 103
- Open Chicken Pot Pie 105
- Chicken and Pancetta Risotto 106
- Sunday Night Chicken Dinner 107
- Pressure Cooker Osos Bunco 109
- Roast Turkey Breast and Gravy 111
- Quick and Easy Korean Beef 112
- Thai Green curry 113
- The Ultimate Beef Taco Bowl 115
- The All-American Meat Loaf 116
- Mediterranean Beef Dinner 117
- Easy Easter Sunday Pot Roast 118
- Ragu Penne Pasta 119
- Spaghetti Squash and Meat Sauce 120
- Spanish Chorizo and Peppers 121
- Country Style Pork Chop Casserole 122
- Pork Medallions and Mushrooms 123
- Herb Garlic Leg of Lamb 124
- Moroccan Lamb and Chickpeas 125
- **Pressure Cooker Seafood Recipes** 126
- Singapore Green Fish Curry 128
- Lemon Pepper Tilapia with Asparagus 129
- Spicy Lemon Salmon 130
- Greek Tuna Noodle Delight 131

Salmon and Scalloped Potatoes	132
Lemon Ginger Mahi-Mahi	133
Shrimp Fried Rice	134
Curry Coconut Cilantro Shrimp	135
Seafood Coconut Curry	136
Milk Fish Curry	138
Clam Linguine	141
Cod Chowder	143
Prawn Risotto	144
Pressure Cooker Crab Legs	145
Pressure Cooker Vegetarian Recipes	**146**
Pressure Cooker Enchilada Quinoa	148
Rustic Vegetable Gratin	149
Swiss Chard with Chickpeas and Couscous	150
Mix Vegetable Curry with Tofu	151
Vegetable Succotash	152
Mixed Vegetable Curry	153
Peas Risotto	154
Asian Crunchy Noodle Salad Bowl	155
Quick Spinach & Corn Au Gratin	156
Pressure Cooker Vegetable Lasagna	157
Homestyle Broccoli and Rice Casserole	159
Easy Veggie Enchilada Orzo	160
Asian Tofu Salad	161
Vegetarian Shepherd's Pie	163
Spinach Tortillas	164
Creamy Mushroom Polenta	165
Vegetarian Tacos	166
Pressure Cooker Dessert Recipes	**167**
Peanut Butter Chocolate Cheesecake	168
Mini Salted Caramel Mocha Cheesecakes	169
Chocolate Fudge	171
Cherry Dump Cake	172

Mango Coconut Rice Pudding	173
Strawberry Pudding	174
Chocolate Peppermint Pudding	175
Mixed Berry Pudding	177
Pumpkin Custard	178
Spiced Apple Crunch	179
French Orange Crème	180
Crème Brule	181
Caramel Custard	182
Stuffed Peaches	183
Apricot Crisp	184
Berry Compote	185
Caramel Fondue	186
Pressure Cooker Bone Broth Stocks	189
Bone and Vegetable Broths	190
Bone Broth	190
Vegetable Broth	190
Your Spice Rack	192
Mediterranean Spice Mix	192
Year Round Vegetables	194
Vegetables in Spring	195
Vegetables in Fall	196
Vegetables in Winter	197
Vegetables in Summer	198

Introduction

Introducing the Pressure Cooker is the perfect appliance for you; in addition to saving you time and effort, it is quite handy and very simple to use and can definitely improve your overall health.

The magic behind how it works is the use of pressurized steam; this cooking method seals most of the nutrients in the cooked meal. Giving you a delicious and juicy home cooked lunch, dinner and even dessert!

The Pressure Cooker is a multi-programmed third generation electric pressure cooker that performs all the functions of a slow cooker, rice cooker, a steamer, a yogurt maker, a sautéing pan and a warming pot, therefore saving you a lot of space and time in your kitchen

This book will provide you with the basic knowledge on how to get the most out of your Pressure Cooker. This book includes some great visuals, such as the knife guide and the conversion table, a pasta guide and even a section on spices too!

The recipes given in this book are easy to follow, healthy and simply heartwarming and delicious. All the recipes have been divided into different categories for your convenience. As you master the recipes, feel free to make adjustments to them and customize them to your liking.

So, let's get started!

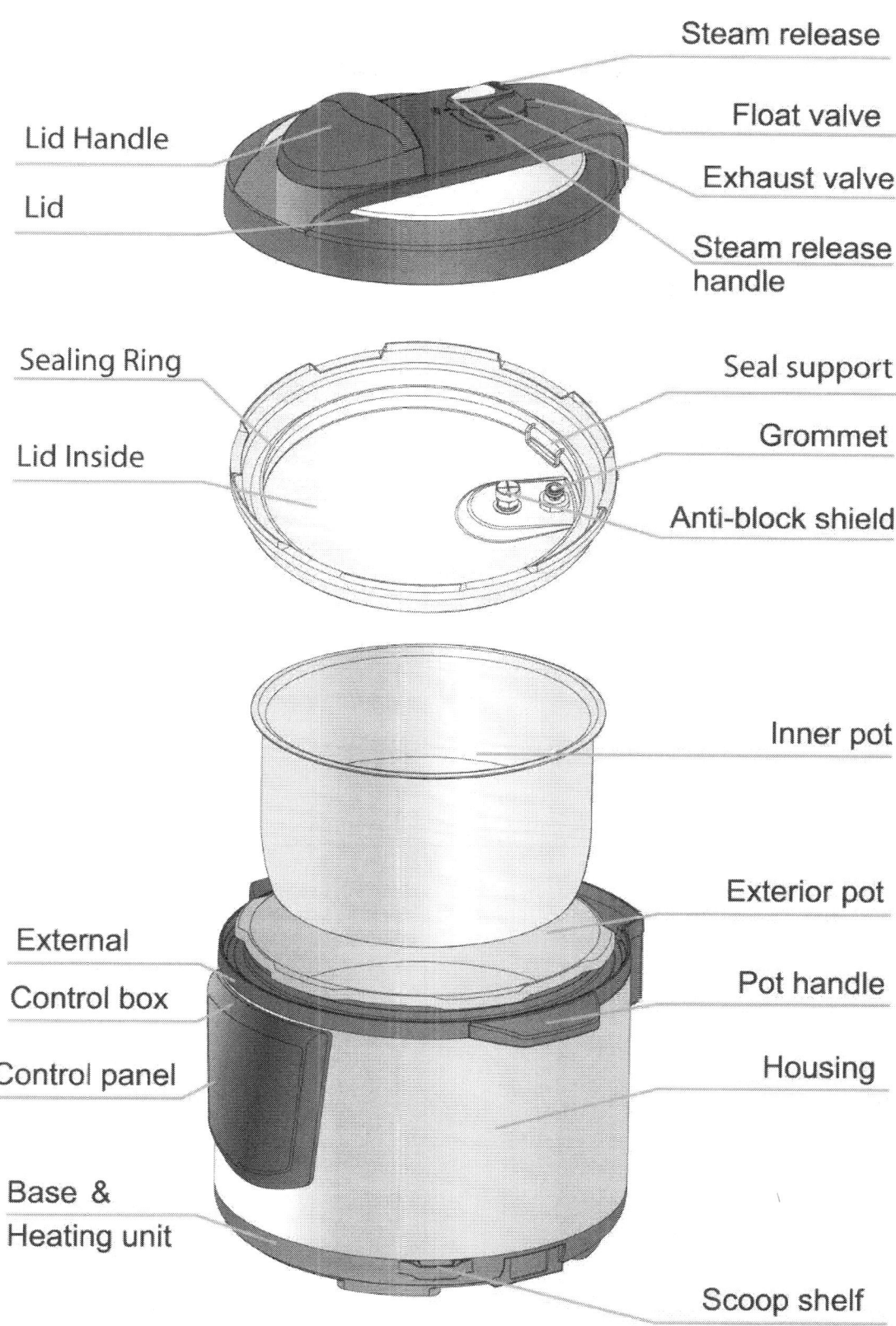

The Inner Pot

The inner pot is detachable, and it is present in the pressure cooker. This high quality grade of stainless steel is quite sturdy and has a copper coating on the bottom for providing uniform heating. The capacity of this part can range from anywhere between 5 to 8 quarts.

Lid

The lid comes along with a gasket that acts as a sealing ring. The lid and the inner pot form an airtight space when the lid is secured on the cooker in a sealed position. This facilitates the increase of pressure within the pot when the amount of heat supplied to the inner pot increases. To prevent the cooker lids from being opened accidentally, electric pressure cookers come along with a pin-lock system, known as the float valve in the Pressure Cooker, which helps in preventing such situations. The Pressure Cooker also has a secondary power switch that is an added safety feature. If the lid has not been secured in the lock position, then the control mechanism of this appliance can detect this condition and will not let the user turn it on for heating.

Safety Valves

Akin to a regular pressure cooker, the pin of the float valve that has been mentioned above can be damaged due to excessive pressure or even temperature. Sans the pin, the float valve becomes a hole for the pressure to escape, and the pressure that's within the compartment will be released through this hole. If that's the case, then the float valve and the lid will have to be replaced for the safe operation of this appliance. The pressure expulsion valve has got several anti-block shields that are present inside the lid and is designed in such a manner that under the usual operating range of pressure, it does not release any pressure when it is in a sealed arrangement.

Housing Unit

The Pressure Cooker has a heating component, a control box, and sensors for reading both pressure and temperature. This control box acts as the functioning and regulating part of the electronic pressure cooker. From the sensors, it monitors the warmth and the pressure that is building up within the inner pot. It has been outfitted with microprocessor that helps in controlling functions like heating, timing, and even the complex cooking functions for which it's been programmed. This positive feedback system helps in creating perfect cooking conditions. Inaudible alarm will be sounded when the microprocessors detect an insecure operating situation and in even more serious situations, the power supply itself can be cut off.

Three Generations of Electric Pressure Cookers

The electric pressure cookers have come a long way since the patent for it was filed for the first time on the9th of January in the year 1991. Based on their capability of controlling the cooking process, they have been classified into three categories or generations.

1st Generation

The first generations of electric pressure cookers are fitted with mechanical timers and the essential sensors for detecting changes in pressure and temperature and act moderator of the threshold limit. If either of the thresholds has been reached, then the power supply tithe heating element is cut off. The only control that is accessible to the user is the mechanical cooking-time controller, which helps in getting an estimate of the cooking duration. The basic safety features and mechanisms like the locking of the lid under pressure, and excess-pressure protection valves have also already been implemented in these cookers.

2nd Generation

The Second Generation Electric Pressure Cookers make use of digital controllers. The pressure sensor has also been connected to the controller electronically, and this means that a countdown timer can be displayed when the working pressure has been reached in the inner pot. The safety features have been further enhanced with the addition of different sensors. The most notable of all these are the improvement made to the lid. If the lid hasn't been fully locked, then the pressure-cooking will not start. This prevents the potential risk of the lid blowing up due to the buildup of pressure.

3rd Generation

The Third Generation Electronic Pressure Cookers refitted with smart programming and have enhanced security features as well. Each of these electric pressure cookers has been fitted with a microprocessor. The accurate readings from the pressure and the temperature sensors, along with the microprocessors can be programmed for performing different cooking tasks and techniques as well. The Smart Programs are fitted for specific cooking purposes by simply varying the intensities of the heat, temperature, pressure, and the time required.

With the advancement in the microprocessor programs, the scope of safety and sophistication has been widened as well. For instance, one common mistake that many make is misplacing the steam release at the open position at the begging of the cooking process. If the steam release is open, then there won't be any steam buildup. Irrespective of this, the earlier generations of cookers would continue the heating process, and if this situation isn't corrected in due course of the cooking, all the liquid that is present in the cooking pot would simply evaporate and ruin the meal. The 3rd Generation cooker comes with a built-in mechanism that is referred to as the Leaky Lid Protection, where the microprocessors help in detecting any excess pre-heating pressure leaks, and would stop the heating period with an alarm if there was.

Reasons for Buying the Pressure Cooker

Cook Beans Super-Fast

This might pique your interest; you can cook beans in less than an hour. Soaked beans can be cooked in 15 to 20 minutes, and dry beans can be cooked within 35 to 40 minutes. Cooking beans has never been this easy.

Make Perfect Brown Rice

Rice isn't easy to cook and to cook it to perfection can be quite challenging. The grain to water ratio that should be made use of in the case of brown rice is 1 to 1.25 and for white rice it's 1 to 1.5. Different Pressure Cooker recipes have been mentioned in this book that you can make use of for cooking different rice-based dishes.

Steam/Cook Veggies in Minutes

Vegetables are probably the most overcooked of the lot. Pressure Cooker makes life so much easier. Vegetables can be steamed or cooked within a few minutes, and the great thing is that, the cooking will stop when you programmed it too as well!

Built in Timer

The Pressure Cooker has a built in timer that won't start cooking till you want it to. You can simply program it to start cooking at 4:30 pm and then keep it warm until the time that you get home.

Easy Clean Up

The Pressure Cooker is quite easy to clean. It comes with a removable stainless steel pot and a lid along with-it. Those two things are the only things that you will have to wash.

Slow Cooker

The Pressure Cooker is almost the same size as a slow cooker, and it does the job of a slow cooker with just the push of button. If you want to make use of your Pressure Cooker as a slow cooker on a regular basis, then make sure that you are purchasing the optional lid along with it as well.

Sauté feature

The Pressure Cooker can also help you in sautéing by simply pressing a button. If you want to, you can toss in onions and garlic, then select the sauté option and get your other ingredients ready till the ones in the Pot are done being sautéed.

Saving Time & Energy

Food can be cooked much faster by pressure-cooking than by any other method of cooking. A Pressure Cooker can help you in reducing your cooking time by 70% when compared to the other methods of cooking. Since much less water is used and it is cooked in a fully insulated pot, much less, energy is required as well when compared to any other cooking technique like boiling or steaming while cooking on a stovetop.

Automatic Cooking

This is convenient and is an automated process. Each cook can be timed and then it would simply switch onto keeping the food warm once it is cooked. Unlike conventional pressure cooker, you needn't stand and monitor the cooking time and process. Delayed Cooking is another fetching feature of the Pressure Cooker. This means that you can plan your meal well ahead of time. You needn't stand around and wait for your meal to be ready. This means that your cooking time is reduced by more than half.

Clean & Pleasant

The Pressure Cooker is quite the opposite of this. The Pressure Cooker is quiet and is fully sealed. The Pressure Cooker will help you in cooking food without heating up the surroundings, and this would be well appreciated during summer time by reducing the electricity required for heating and cooling the food. The Pressure Cooker does help you in keeping your kitchen clean. There won't be any messy spills or splashes, and you don't have to clean up food that boils over. Everything is perfectly sealed and trapped within the inner pot. It is a kitchen-friendly appliance that requires minimal cleaning. It is multipurpose appliance, and it will help in getting rid of the clutter in your kitchen.

Slow cookers cook in a relatively low temperature (at approximately 79°C–93°C or 175°F–200°F range) over a long period of time. Meanwhile, electric pressure cookers run at much higher temperature (over boiling point at 115°C~118°C or 239°F~244°F).

This difference in cooking mechanism results in drastically different cooking time. Typically an electric pressure cooker makes a dish under an hour, whereas the minimal

Energy Efficient

Cooking time for a slow cooker is 4 hours. An Electric pressure cooker saves about 75% electricity comparing to a slow cooker making a similar dish.

Apart from the difference in cooking temperature, there are two other physical differences.

1. **Insulated housing**

Slow cookers typically do not have insulated housing, whereas electric pressure cookers do. This contributes to energy efficiency advantage to electric pressure cookers.

2. **Sealed cooking**

An electric pressure cooker is fully sealed under pressure, letting out no steams and no smells. This is not the case for slow cookers. This makes electric pressure cooker a winner in keeping the kitchen clean and the house smell free.

One disadvantage often cited against slow cookers is that vitamins and other trace nutrients are lost, particularly from vegetables, partially by enzyme action during cooking. When vegetables are cooked at higher temperatures these enzymes are rapidly denatured and have less time in which to act during cooking.

Another disadvantage of slow cookers is that they don't heat the food at a temperature high enough to remove common toxins (for example in raw kidney beans, and some other beans). On the other hand, electric pressure cookers are very good at detoxifying food, owning to its higher than boiling point operating temperature.

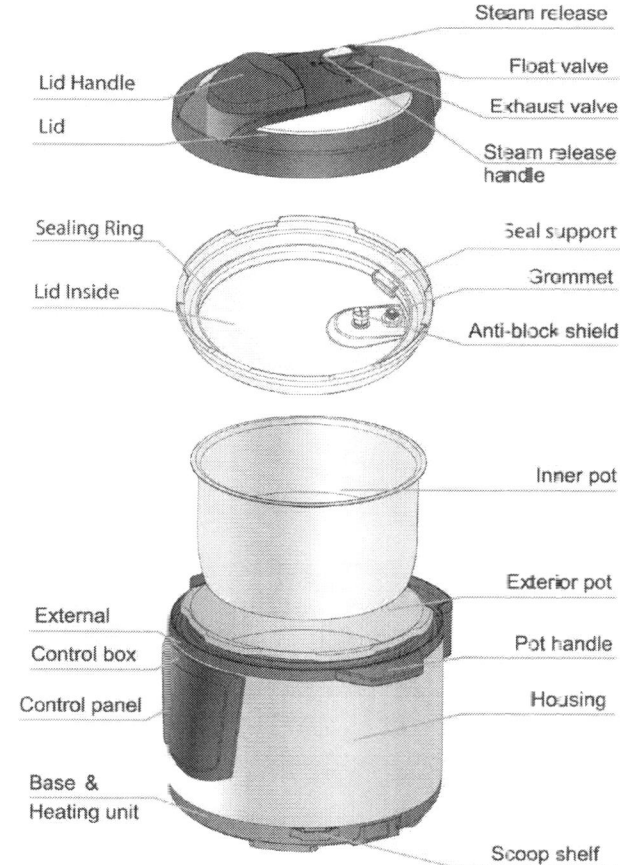

Pressure Release Guide and Terminology

It is always a good idea to read the manual of your Pressure Cooker/Pressure Cooker. The following is a simple guide to get you familiar with the Pressure Release of the Pressure Cooker, followed by a list of terminology that will be useful when you start cooking with your Pressure Cooker.

Quick Pressure Release

This type of release is used to quickly stop the cooking process and prevents overcooking more delicate foods such as leafy green vegetables and certain types of seafood that require very short cooking time. This method is also slightly messier in terms of lots of steam and liquid will get splattered on the roof of your Pressure Cooker lid and may even spill a little into the Exterior Pot. If you use the Quick Pressure Release often, then it is best to clean your Pressure Cooker at a more regular cleaning interval.

Natural Pressure Release

This is a much cleaner method for releasing pressure in your Pressure Cooker, and this is the **method used** in the recipes in this cookbook collection. The Natural Pressure Release gradually releases the pressure inside your Pressure Cooker, therefore less movement and your foods, such as soups, sauces and meats come out cleaner and more intact.

How to Use the Pressure Cooker

By this time, hopefully in front of you lies and Pressure Cooker and you are eager to utilize it to its full potential. The Pressure Cooker is easy to use and we will now commence with sharing the basics of how to use it in six simple steps.

Five Simple Steps to Using Your Pressure Cooker

1. Determine the Duration Required

The first step is simple enough; simply understand how much time you will require to cook your meal. Although it's very simple in meaning, the difference it can make is enormous.

A few minutes undercooked and the flavor isn't quite there, a few minutes overcooked and you'll beating unappealing burnt crisps.

2. Ensure the Lid is ready and clean

Sealing ring is correctly fitted and sterile.
Bloat valve is free of food debris and easily moves up and down.

Steam release handle is clean and the longer part is pointing at the "Sealing" position.
Before cooking any meals, carefully check the above-mentioned steps to ensure the lid is ready for use.

3. Place the Ingredients into the Inner Pot

How difficult can it be to put ingredients into the inner pot? Well, it's not too difficult but there are just 2 points here to watch out for. Alive it could, position your meal into the center with-it touching the edges of the inner pot.

4. Plug Your Pressure Cooker to an Electrical Socket

A beeping sound will occur as your unit gets plugged in; this is step 4, you're almost there!

5. Choose a Function

It's time for the fun part; using this all-in-one machine, you can make such a large combination of meals and it's exciting to learn the different functions! We'll go over each of the functions here for you and how to use them.

The control Panel on a Pressure Cooker

The Functions

Soup

Default Time: 30 minutes

Adjust: 40 minutes or 20 minutes

Pressure Setting: High Pressure

Poultry

Default Time: 15 minutes

Adjust: 30 minutes or 5 minutes

Pressure Setting: High Pressure

Meat/Stew

Default Time: 35 minutes

Adjust: 45 minutes or 20 minutes

Pressure Setting: High Pressure

Bean/Chili

Default Time: 30 minutes

Adjust: 40 minutes or 25 minutes

Pressure Setting: High Pressure

Sauté

Used with lid off

Adjust: Less (Simmer), More (Brown)

Rice

Automatically adjusts time duration depending on the ratio of water to rice.

Adjust: Non-adjustable

Pressure Setting: Low

Multi-grain

Default Time: 40 minutes

Adjust: 60 minutes or 20 minutes

Pressure Setting: High Pressure

Congee/Porridge

Default Time: 20 minutes

Adjust: 30 minutes or 15 minutes

Pressure Setting: High Pressure

Steam

Default Time: 10 minutes

Adjust: 15 minutes or 3 minutes

Pressure Setting: High Pressure

Note: Use a wire rack or steamer basket

Slow Cook

Default Time: 4 hours

Adjust: Low temperature or high temperature

Time Adjustments: Through utilizing the "+" and "-", you may adjust the cooking time

Yogurt

The Yogurt function in the Pressure Cooker is unique amongst electric pressure cookers and is another reason why people choose the Pressure Cooker.

Manual

This function will allow you to choose your desired time. The maximum limit is 120 minutes. In the case that you have a certain time that isn't part of any "pre-set "functions, you can use this.

Adjust

This button allows you to change any of the "pre-set "functions to their adjustable settings.

Timer

This function allows you to delay the cook start time bay maximum limit of 24 hours.

Keep Warm

As a general rule, this feature should always be kept on, unless specific recipes call for it. What this does is keep your cooked meal warm for up to 10 hours in the event that you forgot or had to step out of the house.

Depressurizing Your Pressure Cooker

Once your meal is finished cooking, you'll have to get rid of the pressure in the Pressure Cooker. There are two methods to release the pressure.

Natural Release

To perform a natural release, all you have to do is turn off your Pressure Cooker and wait between 5 to 20 minutes depending on how much pressure is within the pot.

Quick Release

To perform a quick release, simply turn the steam release handle either to the left or right. An important note to make here is that when performing a quick release, use towel or a cooking mitt; the hot steam that is released can cause serious burns, as it will be extremely hot.

Sautéing

All the present Pressure Cooker models have a sauté; this is a feature that even a slow cooker doesn't have. The Pressure Cooker is a one-pot marvel, and you can make use of it as stovetop skillet before switching over to the pressure cooker function. It is quite a flawless transition. All the recipes provided in this book are guaranteed to blow your mind.

Safety Features

Most of the pressure cooker accidents that occurred in the past can be attributed the error committed on part of the user. The Pressure Cooker has been designed in such fashion that it will help in getting rid of and avoiding most of the human error threats that plagued the former models. The Pressure Cooker has been developed by one of the top manufacturers of electric pressure cookers, and all the Pressure Cookers available for sale have been certified by UL/ULC.

The pressure sensor helps in controlling the amount of power and heating that should be maintained within the present in the Pressure Cooker. The pressure sensor, like its name suggests, helps in maintaining the pressure build up in the Pressure Cooker to avoid any accidents.

Apart from this ingenious safety feature, here are the ten safety features that are built into the Pressure Cooker.

Feature#1: Lid Close Detection

If the lid of the Pressure Cooker hasn't been closed properly, then the appliance will not be able to activate its function of pressurized cooking. If the lid if even partially open, the only functions that would work are the keep-warm and the sauté options.

Feature#2: Leaky Lid Protection

If the cooker lid has any leakage in it, the cooker will not be able to reach the optimum present level of pressure. The leakage could be caused because of a variety of reasons such as if the stem release hasn't been properly closed, or perhaps if the sealing ring isn't fully sealed. If this function weren't enabled, then this could lead to the burning of your food. The Pressure Cooker helps in detecting this by taking note of the time taken for pre-heating. If the pre-heating process were taking longer than usual, then the programming would automatically switch the Pressure Cooker onto the Keep-warm feature for avoiding the food from getting burnt.

Feature#3: Lid Lock under Pressure

To prevent the accidental opening of the cooker, the lid will remain locked to make sure that the cooker is pressurized properly.

Feature#4: Anti-blockage Vent

It is very likely that during the cooking process, certain food particles could restrict the release of the steam by jamming the vent. The Pressure Cooker has a vent shield that has been specifically structured to avoid the jamming of the steam vent.

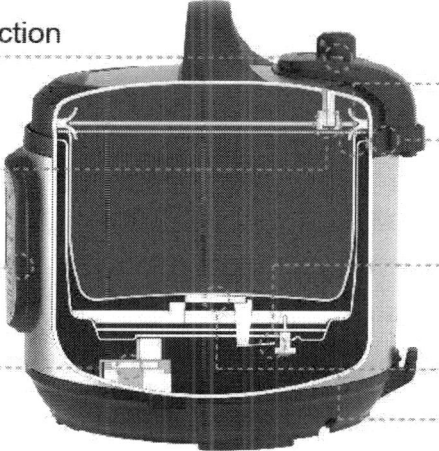

Pressure Regulator Protection

Anti-Blockage Vent

Leaky Lid Protection

Extreme Temperature & Power Protection

Excess Pressure Protection

Safety Lid Lock

Automatic Pressure Control

Automatic Temperature Control

High Temperature Warning

Feature#5: Automatic Temperature Control

The thermostat that is present under the inner pot of the Pressure Cooker helps in regulating the temperature of thinner pot and makes certain that it is within a safe range depending upon the type of food that is being cooked.

Feature#6: High-Temperature Warning

If the cooker is functioning without sufficient water or moisture, then there won't be sufficient pressure build upon the pot, and the cooking process would halt. The most likely outcome of this would be overheating. Excessive temperature might also occur due to different situations such as where the inner pot is missing, not in proper contact with the heating element of the cooker or perhaps the inner pot has got a heat-dissipating problem. The problem of heat dissipation in the inner pot can because if there is burnt starch at the lining of the inner pot that's blocking the heat. In such conditions, the Pressure Cooker will simply stop heating when the temperature has reached a certain limit.

Feature#7: Temperature and Power Protection

The Pressure Cooker has been equipped with a particular fuse that will disconnect itself when the power has reached a high temperature; that is anywhere between 169°C to172°C or 336°F to 341.6°F or if there's an extremely high electrical current passing through. An unusually high electrical current if drawn by the cooker points out an unsafe condition.

Feature #8: Automatic Pressure Control

The Pressure Cooker comes with a patented pressure sensor mechanism that ensures that the operating pressure of this appliance doesn't exceed the range of 70kPa to80kPa or 10.12psi to 11.6psi.

Feature#9: Pressure Regulator Protection

If the pressure in the Pressure Cooker goes beyond 105kPa or15.23 psi, then the steam release will be pushed aside tallow for the excess steam to be pushed out of the inner pot and for lowering the excess pressure that has been building up in the pot. This is similar to the function of the pressure regulators that are present in a stovetop pressure cooker.

Feature#10: Excess Pressure Protection

If the pressure gets too high and this caused the pressure regulator protection that has been mentioned in the previous point to malfunction, then the internal protection mechanism present in the Pressure Cooker will be activated, and this shifts the inner pot downwards so that gap is created between the lid and the inner pot. This will help in the release of steam from the internal chamber and stop the excessive heating.

Conversion Chart

Butter

1 Stick	4 ounces	8 tablespoons	½ cup

Lemon

1 Lemon	1 to 3 tablespoons juice	1 to 1 ½ teaspoons grated zest
4 Large Lemons	1 cup juice	¼ cup grated zest

Creams

Half and Half	½ milk ½ cream	11-18% butter fat
Light cream		18% butter fat
Heavy Cream	Whipping cream	36% or more butter fat
Double Cream	Clotted or Devonshire	42% butter fat

Cooking Conversion Chart

Unit:	Equals:	Also equals:	Metric Equivialant
1 tsp.	1/6 fl. oz.	1/3 Tbsp.	5 mL
1 Tbsp.	1/2 fl. oz.	3 tsp.	15 mL
1/8 cup	1 fl. oz.	2 Tbsp.	30 mL
1/4 cup	2 fl. oz.	4 Tbsp.	60 mL
1/3 cup	2 3/4 fl. oz.	1/4 cup plus 4 tsp.	80 mL
1/2 cup	4 fl. oz.	8 Tbsp.	120 mL
2/3 cup	5 1/2 fl. oz.	1/2 cup plus 2 T + 2 tsp.	160 mL
1 cup	8 fl. oz.	1/2 pint	240 mL
1 pint	16 fl. oz.	2 cups	475 mL
1 quart	32 fl. oz.	2 pints (4 cups)	950 mL
1 liter	34 fl. oz.	1 quart plus 1/4 cup	1 L
1 gallon	128 fl. oz.	4 quarts	3.8 L
1 lb	16 oz.	0.45359237 kg	

Note: In cases where higher precision is not justified, it may be convenient to round these conversions off as follows:

1 cup = 250 mL   1 pint = 500 mL   1 quart = 1 L   1 gallon = 4 L

PRESSURE COOKER ACCESSORES

1. Extra Silicone Sealing Rings

- **Silicone Sealing Ring** – Pressure Cooker Sealing Rings' life expectancy varies. If steam starts to leak around the lid, replace the Pressure Cooker Sealing Ring immediately.
- **Genuine Sweet & Savory Edition Silicone Sealing Ring – Two Pack** – Since the sealing ring will absorb the smell of the food in the pot, many users also like to use separate sealing rings for cooking savory dishes and desserts.

2. Steamer Racks

- **Stainless Steel Steaming Rack Stand 5" Diameter** – this is the most commonly used accessory for cooking in Pressure Cooker. *A must for using the Pot-In-Pot method!*
- **Stainless Steel Steamer Basket** – Another steamer basket we use frequently.

3. **Containers** – any oven-safe containers will be safe to use in the Pressure Cooker.

All about Beans and Legumes

LEGUME	ELECTRIC PRESSURE COOKER (10-12PSI) DRY	STOVETOP PRESSURE COOKER (13-15PSI) DRY	ELECTRIC PRESSURE COOKER (10-12PSI) SOAKED *	STOVETOP PRESSURE COOKER (13-15PSI) SOAKED *	PRESSURE SELECTION	OPENING METHOD
Adzuki or Azuki, red and green	20	15	9	5	High	Natural
Anasazi	22	20	7	4	High	Natural
Black Beans	24	22	6	4	High	Natural
Black-eyed Peas	7	6	5	3	High	Natural
Borlotti	25	20	10	7	High	Natural
Cannellini	30	25	8	6	High	Natural
Chickpeas	40	35	15	13	High	Natural
Chickpeas, split	7	5	-	-		
Chole (see Chickpeas)						
Corona	30	25	10	8	High	Natural
Cranberry (see Borlotti)						
Fava, dried	30	25	12	10	High	Natural
Fava, fresh	8	6	-	-	High	Normal, Natural
Flageolet (see Navy)						
Garbanzo (see Chickpeas)						
Giant White Beans (see Corona or Lima)						
Great Northern Beans (see Cannellini)						
Green Beans (see VEGETABLES)						
Harticots (see Cannellini)						
Kidney Bean, white (see Cannellini)						
Lentils, Black Beluga	8	7			High	Natural
Lentils, French Green, green, or mini	10	8	5	7	High	Natural
Lentils, Split - Red, Orange, or Yellow	1	1	-	-	High	Natural
Lima, baby or large	15	12	7	5	High	Natural
Lobia (see Black-eyed Peas)						
Masoor (see Peas, split)						
Mung (see Adzuki, green)	8	6				
Navy	20	18	8	6	High	Natural
Peanuts, Fresh			50	45	High	Natural
Peas, white (see Navy)						
Peas, whole green	18	16	10	8	High	Natural
Peas, split, green	5	5	-	-	High	Natural
Peas, split, yellow or orange (see Lentils, split)						

Pressure Cooker Breakfast Recipes

Lemon Blueberry Steel Cut Oats

Servings: 4

Total time taken: 25

Ingredients:

- 2 cups steel cut oats
- 6 cups water
- 2 tablespoons lemon zest, grated
- 2 tablespoons butter
- 1 cup half and half
- 4 tablespoons sugar or sweetener of your choice to taste
- 2 cups blueberries, fresh or frozen
- ½ cup chia seeds

Directions:

1. Switch on the Pressure Cooker and select the Sauté option. Add butter to the cooking pot.
2. When the butter melts, add oats and stir well until the oats are lightly toasted.
3. Add water, half and half, sugar, salt and lemon zest and mix well. Lock lid of the pot. Select the Multi-grain option and Adjust down to 20 minutes. Set timer, once timer goes off quick release pressure.
4. Add blueberries and chia seeds. Mix well. Serve with milk and maple syrup and sliced almonds.

Oatmeal Apple Crisp

Servings: 6

Total time taken: 20 min

Ingredients:

- 6 cups red apples, peeled, sliced
- 1 ½ cups quick cooking oats
- 1 tablespoons lemon juice
- ¼ cup flour
- ¾ cup brown sugar
- ¼ cup butter, melted
- 1 ½ teaspoons cinnamon
- ¾ teaspoon salt
- 2 ½ cups water

Directions:

1. Sprinkle lemon juice over the cut apples. Mix together oats, flour, sugar, salt, margarine and cinnamon.
2. Take a greased tin or metal bowl that is smaller than the cooker and fits in the pot. Place a layer of apples next layer with the oats mixture. Repeat the layers until the apples is the topmost layer. Cover the tin with aluminum foil.
3. Switch on the Pressure Cooker and pour water in it. Place a rack inside the pot and place bowl on the rack.
4. Close the lid and select the Multi-grain function and Adjust down to 20 minutes.
5. Quick release the pressure. Serve warm.

Chocolate Chip French toast

Servings: 4

Total time taken: 30 minutes

Ingredients:

- 6 cups French bread, cubed
- 1 cup milk
- 2 eggs
- 1 teaspoon vanilla extract
- 1/3 cup semi-sweet chocolate chips
- 1/3 cup packed brown sugar
- 1 teaspoon ground cinnamon

Directions:

1. Grease the inside of the cooking pot with oil. Place bread at the bottom of the pot.
2. Whisk together eggs, milk, sugar, vanilla and cinnamon in a bowl and pour over the bread. Stir well.
3. Top with chocolate chips. Switch on the Pressure Cooker.
4. Lock lid. Select the Slow Cook function and set the timer for 30 minutes. Once timer goes off, quick release pressure and serve warm with a drizzle of honey.

Creamy Cheesy Grits

Servings: 2-3

Total time taken: 15-20 min

Ingredients:

- ½ cup stone ground grits
- 1 cup half and half
- 1 cup water
- 8 ounces cheddar cheese
- 2 tablespoons butter
- 1 ½ cups water
- 2 tablespoons olive oil

Directions:

1. Switch on the Pressure Cooker.
2. Set the Sauté function. Add oil and grits and toast lightly. Press Cancel button.
3. Add rest of the ingredients.
4. Lock the lid. Select the Manual option and set timer for 10 minutes.
5. Let the pressure release naturally for 15 minutes and quick release excess pressure.

Breakfast Burrito

Servings: 3

Total time taken: 15 min

Ingredients:

- 1½ tablespoons olive oil
- 6 eggs, boiled, peeled, diced
- 1/3 cup tomatoes, diced
- 1 medium onion, diced
- 3 tablespoons fresh cilantro, chopped
- ¾ cup cooked black beans, warmed
- Salt to taste
- Pepper powder to taste
- 3 large tortillas, warmed
- 1 medium avocado, peeled, pitted, diced
- 1/3 cup water
- 3 tablespoons sour cream
- 3 tablespoons cheddar cheese, shredded

Directions:

1. Switch on the Pressure Cooker and select the Sauté function.
2. Add olive oil. Sauté for a couple of minute's and add onions, tomatoes, cilantro, water and salt. Lock lid. Select the Poultry function and Adjust down to 15 minutes.
3. When the timer goes off, release the pressure with quick release.
4. Place the tortillas on your work area. Divide the egg mixture among the tortillas. Divide the beans and place over the egg mixture. Place some avocado slices in the center.
5. Spread a tablespoon of sour cream. Sprinkle cheese. Roll and serve.

Cheesy Egg Bake

Servings: 6

Total time taken: 15 min

Ingredients:

- 12 eggs
- 9 slices bacon, chopped
- 1 cup mushrooms, sliced
- 1 red bell pepper, chopped
- 1 green bell pepper, chopped
- 1 yellow bell pepper, chopped
- 2 green onions, chopped
- 1½ cups cheddar cheese
- 3 cups frozen hash browns
- 1/3 cup milk

Directions:

1. Select the Sauté function and add bacon. Cook until crisp. Add hash browns and sauté for 2 minutes.
2. Whisk together rest of the ingredients in a bowl except for green onions and pour into the pot.
3. Cover and select the Poultry option and Adjust down to 15 minutes.
4. Sprinkle green onions and cheese then serve.

Vegan Quiche

Servings: 4

Total time taken: 25 min

Ingredients:

- 20 ounces frozen spinach, thawed, squeezed of excess moisture
- 1 cup onions, chopped
- 16 ounces mushrooms, sliced
- 28 ounces firm tofu, press to remove excess moisture
- 4 cloves garlic, minced
- 4 tablespoons nutritional yeast
- 1 teaspoon dried basil
- 1 teaspoon dried thyme
- ½ teaspoon pepper powder
- ½ teaspoon red pepper flakes
- 2 tablespoons olive oil
- 2 tablespoons apple cider vinegar
- 2 tablespoons lemon juice
- 2 teaspoons lemon zest, grated
- Cooking spray

Directions:

1. Spray the inside of the cooking pot with cooking spray.
2. Switch on the Pressure Cooker. Select the Sauté function. Add oil, garlic, onions, spinach, and mushrooms.
3. Add salt, pepper, and basil, and thyme, chili flakes. Sauté for a few seconds.
4. Blend together tofu, lemon zest and juice, and vinegar until smooth. Pour into the pot.
5. Add nutritional yeast and fold. Press the Cancel button.
   Close the lid. Select the Slow Cook function and set the timer for 25 minutes.
   Cut into wedges and serve.

No Crust Quiche

Servings: 4

Total time taken: 60 min

Ingredients:

- 9 eggs, well beaten
- ¾ cup milk
- ¼ teaspoon pepper powder or to taste
- ½ teaspoon salt or to taste
- ¾ cup ham, diced
- 1 cup ground sausage, cooked
- 6 slices bacon, cooked, crumbled
- 3 large green onions, sliced
- 2 cups cheese, shredded

Directions:

1. Whisk together in a bowl, eggs, milk, salt and pepper.
2. Place bacon, sausage, ham, green onions and cheese in a soufflé dish. Mix well. Pour beaten egg mixture over it. Mix until well combined. Cover the dish with aluminum foil.
3. Place a metal trivet at the bottom of the cooking pot. Add 1 cup of water. Place the dish over the trivet. Switch on the Pressure Cooker.
4. Close the lid and select the bean/chili option and use the default time of 30 minutes.
5. When the timer goes off, let the steam release naturally for 10 minutes and then release the pressure with a quick release.
6. Remove the dish from the pot and discard the foil. Serve immediately.

Mexican Breakfast Casserole

Servings: 6

Total time taken: 1.5 hrs.

Ingredients:

- 12 eggs
- 2 pounds bulk chorizo, cooked, drained
- 2 cups milk
- 12 corn tortillas
- 1 large red bell pepper, chopped
- 2 jalapeños, finely chopped
- 1 cup green onions, chopped
- 1½ cups chunky salsa
- 1½ cup pepper Jack cheese, shredded
- ¼ cup fresh cilantro

Directions:

1. Spray the cooking pot with cooking spray.
2. Whisk together in a bowl, eggs, salt, pepper and milk.
3. Retain about 2 tablespoons each of green onions and red bell peppers and ½ cup cheese and set the rest aside for layering.
4. Place 3 tortillas at the bottom of the Pressure Cooker. Place 1/3 the chorizo over it followed by 1/3 bell pepper, 1/3 red bell pepper and 1/3 the cheese.
5. Repeat the above steps. Place the remaining 3 tortillas over it. Pour the egg mixture over it.
6. Switch on the Pressure Cooker. Lock lid. Select the Slow Cook function and set the timer for 1.5 hours.
7. Garnish with cilantro, green onion, bell pepper, and cheese and serve with salsa.

Breakfast Hash

Servings: 6

Total time taken: 20 min

Ingredients:

- 8 medium potatoes, peeled, shredded, squeeze excess moisture out
- 12 eggs, beaten
- 2 cups bacon, cooked, crumbled
- 2 cups cheese, grated
- ½ cup water
- Cooking spray

Directions:

1. Spray the inside of the cooking pot with cookingspray. Select the Sauté function and add potatoes and sauté until brown.
2. Add rest of the ingredients and stir.
3. Switch on the Pressure Cooker. Lock lid. Select the Steam function and Adjust down to 10 minutes.
4. Stir and serve with toast.

Pressure Cooker Sauce Recipes

HOW TO MIX YOUR OWN SEASONING

HOMEMADE LEMON PEPPER

- 2 tablespoon lemon zest
- 3 tablespoon ground black pepper
- 1 tablespoon salt

HOMEMADE ITALIAN SEASONING

- ¼ cup dried basil
- 2 tablespoon dried thyme
- 2 tablespoon dried marjoram
- 2 tablespoon dried rosemary
- 2 tablespoon dried oregano
- 2 tablespoon garlic powder
- 2 tablespoon dried coriander
- 1 tsp sugar

HOMEMADE POULTRY SEASONING

- 2 tablespoon sage
- 1 ½ tablespoon thyme
- 1 tablespoon marjoram
- ¾ tablespoon rosemary
- ½ tablespoon nutmeg
- ½ tablespoon black pepper

HOMEMADE TACO SEASONING

- 6 tablespoon chili powder
- 4 ½ tablespoon cumin
- 3 tablespoon onion powder
- 2 ½ tablespoon garlic powder
- 5 tablespoon paprika
- ¼ tablespoon cayenne pepper
- ¼ tablespoon oregano

Fresh Tomato Sauce

Servings: 4-6

Total time taken: 4 hrs. 15 min

Ingredients:

- 13 medium tomatoes, diced
- 6 cloves garlic, peeled, minced
- 2 medium carrots, diced
- 2 medium onions, diced
- 4 bay leaves
- 2 cups vegetable broth
- 3 tablespoons olive oil
- 3 tablespoons Italian seasoning
- 3 teaspoons pepper powder
- 1 ½ tablespoons red pepper flakes
- 1 ½ teaspoons salt

Directions:

1. Add all the ingredients to the inner pot and stir well.
2. Switch on the Pressure Cooker. Lock lid. Select the Slow Cook function and use the default time of 4 hours.
3. When cool enough to handle, ladle into blender and blend until smooth.
4. Use as required. If you need to store it, then place in freezer safe containers and freeze. Keeps for up to a month.

Ragu (Meat Sauce)

Servings: 6

Total time taken: 20-30 min

Ingredients:

- 18 ounces Italian sausage, discard casing
- 2 cloves garlic, peeled
- 1 large red onion, chopped
- 2 cans (14 ounces each) chopped tomatoes
- 1 tablespoon dried oregano
- Salt and pepper to taste

Directions:

1. Select the Sauté function. Add sausage and cook until light brown.
2. Add the rest of the ingredients and stir. Simmer until the liquid dries up.
3. Once liquid is reduced the sauce is ready, distribute into jars or in freezer safe containers.

Italian Spaghetti Meat Sauce

Servings: 12

Total time taken: 4 hrs. 15 min

Ingredients:

- 1 cup onion, chopped
- 1 pound Italian pork sausage or ground beef
- 2 cloves garlic, finely chopped
- 1 cup fresh mushrooms, sliced
- 14 ounces canned diced tomatoes, with liquid
- ½ a 6 ounce can tomato paste
- 1 can (15 ounces) tomato sauce
- ½ tablespoon sugar
- 1 tablespoon dried basil leaves
- Salt to taste
- Pepper powder to taste
- 1 teaspoon dried oregano
- ½ teaspoon red pepper flakes

Directions:

1. Switch on the Pressure Cooker. Select the Sauté function and press Adjust once for more heat.
2. Add onions, mushrooms, garlic and sausages and cook until pink. Press the Cancel button. Drain the excess fat and discard. Add the rest of the ingredients.
3. Close the lid. Select the Slow Cook function and use the default time of 4 hours.
4. Once time is up, you can use this for pasta, rice or even over baked potatoes. Freeze the remaining sauce in freezer safe containers.

Ball Game Hot Dog Sauce

Servings: 12

Total time taken: 3 hrs.

Ingredients:

- 2 pounds ground beef
- ½ teaspoon garlic, minced
- 1 cup onions, chopped
- 1 cup water
- 30 ounces tomato sauce
- 2 teaspoons chili powder
- 2 teaspoons salt

Directions:

1. Add all the ingredients to the inner pot. Switch on the Pressure Cooker.
2. Lock the lid. Select the Slow Cook function and set the timer for 3 hours.
3. Quick release pressure, season sauce to taste then transfer into an airtight container and refrigerate until use.

Mediterranean Eggplant Sauce

Servings: 12

Total time taken: 4 hrs. 15 min

Ingredients:

- 2 pounds eggplant, cut into cubes
- 4 cloves garlic, chopped
- 1 large onion, chopped
- 4 cans (14½ ounce each) diced tomatoes
- 2 cans (6 ounce each) Italian tomato paste
- 8 ounces mushrooms, sliced
- ½ cup water
- ½ cup red wine
- 3 teaspoons dried oregano
- Pepper powder to taste
- Salt to taste

Directions:

1. Add all the ingredients into the inner pot. Switch on the Pressure Cooker.
2. Close the lid. Select the Slow Cook option and use the default time of 4 hours.
3. Serve over pasta garnished with olives, parsley and cheese.

Tomato Basil Sauce

Servings: 6-8

Total time taken: 20 min

Ingredients:

- 2 ½ pounds Roma tomatoes, chopped
- 1 onion, chopped
- 4 cloves garlic, minced
- 2 tablespoons olive oil
- 1 teaspoon garlic powder
- 1 bay leaf
- 1 teaspoon salt
- 1 teaspoon pepper
- 1 teaspoon crushed pepper
- 2 teaspoons Italian seasoning
- ¼ cup fresh basil, roughly chopped

Directions:

1. Switch on the Pressure Cooker. Select the Sauté function. Add oil, onions and garlic and sauté until translucent. Press the Cancel button. Add rest of the ingredients except basil.
2. Close the lid. Select the Steam function adjust the timer down to 20 minutes. Set timer, once timer goes off let it naturally release pressure. Mix basil and use.

Marinara Sauce

Servings: 10-12

Total time taken: 50 min

Ingredients:

- 10 medium tomatoes roughly chopped
- ½ cup red lentils, rinsed
- 3 cups sweet potatoes, cubed
- 5 cloves garlic, minced
- 1½ teaspoons salt
- 2½ cups vegetable broth

Directions:

1. Add all ingredients to the inner pot and stir well. Switch on the Pressure Cooker.
2. Lock lid and cook on High for 40 minutes. Let it naturally release. Then when cooled, add the tomato mixture to a blender and roughly pulse it for 8 minutes.
3. Let cool. Pour into a jar and refrigerate until use.

Pressure Cooker Pizza Sauce

Servings: 10-12

Total time taken: 15-20 min

Ingredients:

- 2 pounds Roma tomatoes, chopped
- ¼ cup garlic, minced
- ¼ cup olive oil
- 1 teaspoon dried oregano
- 2 teaspoons salt
- ½ teaspoon red pepper flakes

Directions:

1. Switch on the Pressure Cooker.
2. Select the Sauté function. Add oil. When the oils heated, add garlic and sauté until golden brown taking care not to brown it. Add the rest of the ingredients and stir. Press the Cancel button.
3. Lock the lid. Select the Manual option and set the timer for 15 minutes. Let the pressure release naturally. Transfer into an airtight container. Drizzle oil and stir. Refrigerate until use.

Pressure Cooker Bolognese Sauce

Servings: 10-12

Total time taken: 4 hrs. 15 min

Ingredients:

- 1½ pounds ground turkey
- 1½ cans (28 ounces each) tomato puree
- 3 small carrots, chopped
- 1 large onion, chopped
- 5 cloves garlic, minced
- 9 ounces canned tomato paste
- 1½ tablespoons olive oil
- ¼ teaspoon crushed red pepper flakes
- 3 teaspoons Italian herb blend
- ¾ teaspoon pepper powder
- ½ teaspoons sea salt
- ¾ cup chicken stock

Directions:

1. Switch on the Pressure Cooker. Place turkey meat in the inner pot.
2. Whisk the rest of the ingredients together in a bowl. Pour over the turkey. Cover and select the Slow Cook function and set the timer for the default time of 4 hours.
3. When done, mash with a potato masher and use as required. Refrigerate the rest or portion it into freezer safe containers and freeze. Keeps well up to 4 weeks.

Pressure Cooker Soups Stews Recipes

Cream of Chicken Mushroom Soup

Servings: 6

Total time taken: 30 min

Ingredients:

- 1 tablespoon olive oil
- 8 ounces boneless, skinless chicken thighs, cut into 1-inch chunks
- Kosher salt and freshly ground black pepper
- 2 tablespoons butter
- 3 cloves garlic, minced
- 8 ounces cremini mushrooms, thinly sliced
- 1 onion, diced
- 3 carrots, peeled and diced
- 2 stalks celery, diced
- ½ teaspoon dried thyme
- ¼ cup all-purpose flour
- 4 cups chicken stock
- 1 bay leaf
- ½ cup half and half
- 2 tablespoons chopped fresh parsley leaves
- 1 sprig fresh rosemary

Directions:

1. Heat olive oil in pressure cooker inner pot. Season chicken thighs with salt and pepper. Add chicken to the pot and Sauté each side until golden, about 2-3 minutes; set aside.

2. Melt butter in the inner pot Add garlic, mushrooms, onion, carrots and celery. Sauté until tender, about 3-4 minutes. Stir in thyme until fragrant, about 1 minute.
3. Whisk in flour until lightly browned, about 1 minute. Whisk in chicken stock, bay leaf and chicken thighs, and cook, whisking constantly, until slightly thickened, about 4-5 minutes.
4. Stir in half and half until heated through, about 1-2 minutes; season with salt and pepper, to taste. If the soup is too thick, add more half and half as needed until desired consistency. Serve immediately.

Add Your Own Tips & Tricks

Chicken Vegetable Soup

Servings: 6

Total time taken: 35 min

Ingredients:

- 1¼ pounds sliced carrots
- 1 pound sliced celery
- 1 pound sliced leeks, white and green parts
- 1 pound chicken breasts, cut into ½-inch pieces
- 3 tablespoons extra-virgin olive oil
- 2 teaspoons sea salt
- A handful of fresh thyme
- 4 cups chicken broth

Directions:

1. Press the Sauté button on the Pressure Cooker, bring it to High, and add olive oil. When the pan is hot, add chicken and sauté for 5 minutes, stirring frequently. Add vegetables, sea salt, thyme, and broth.
2. Lock the lid. Press Manual for High pressure. Set the cooking time to 25 minutes. Once time is up, quick release the pressure. Open the lid and discard thyme.
3. Check seasoning and adjust salt to taste. Serve hot.

Spanish Sardines and Tomato Soup

Servings: 2

Total time taken: 20 min

Ingredients:

- 2 tablespoons olive oil
- 1 tablespoon crushed garlic
- 1 white onion, chopped
- 1 large tomato sliced
- Spanish sardines - 1 (4 3/8 ounce) tin, in tomato sauce and olive oil
- 3 cup fish stock
- 2 cups baby spinach leaves
- Salt and pepper to taste

Directions:

1. Press Sauté button and add olive oil and sauté the garlic and onions and tomato for 5 minutes. Add in the sardines, and fish stock.
2. Lock lid and cook on High pressure for 20 minutes. Once timer is up quick release pressure. Stir in baby spinach leaves.
3. Serve with salt and pepper to taste and lemon wedges on the side.

Creamy Crab Soup

Serving: 4

Total time taken: 20 min

Ingredients:

- 4 tablespoons unsalted butter, divided
- 1 large white onion, diced
- ¼ teaspoon celery salt
- ¼ teaspoon Worcestershire sauce
- 1 pound blue crab meat
- ½ teaspoon sea salt
- 1 teaspoon black pepper, freshly ground
- 2 cups fish stock
- 3 cups milk,
- 1 cup heavy cream
- 1 tablespoon sherry
- 2 tablespoons chives, sliced

Directions:

1. Press Sauté button on Pressure Cooker and add the butter and quickly sauté the diced onion with butter. Then add the Worcestershire sauce, and celery salt; mix well.
2. Then add the crab meat and stir and add the fish stock, cream and milk. Lock lid and cook on High for 20 minutes. Once timer is up quick release pressure.
3. Stir in the sherry sea salt and pepper. Taste and adjust the seasoning to your liking. Pour into warm soup bowls and garnish with fresh chives.

Vegetable Hamburger Soup

Serving: 4

Total time taken: 40 min

Ingredients:

- 2 pounds ground beef
- 2 cups chopped onion
- 2 cups diced potatoes
- 2 cups diced carrots
- 2 cups shredded cabbage
- 2 (14.5 oz.) cans of diced tomatoes
- 2 (14.5 oz.) cans of tomato sauce
- ½ tablespoon ground mustard
- 6 cups beef broth
- Shredded cheese for garnish
- Chopped dill pickles

Directions:

1. Select sauté on and brown meat with a little bit of olive oil. Then add in the onions and sauté for another 5 minutes.
2. Add in the rest of your ingredients, not including the cheese and dill pickles.
3. Select the Soup option and keep it at 30 minutes.
4. Once time is up let the soup naturally release pressure for 15-20 minutes.
5. Top with shredded cheese and chopped dill pickles.

Hearty Beef Quinoa Soup

Serving: 4

Total time taken: 45 min

Ingredients:

- 7 scallions, chopped
- 2 cloves garlic, minced
- 1 tomato, diced
- 1 teaspoon cumin
- 1 pound beef, cubed into small bite size pieces
- 6 cups beef broth
- 1 carrot, peeled and sliced
- 2 yellow bell pepper, diced
- 2 medium potatoes, peeled and cubed
- 1 cup cooked quinoa
- ½ cup chopped cilantro

Directions:

1. On Sauté add in scallions and garlic and sauté until soft, about 3 minutes. Then add your beef and sauté until brown. Then add in the rest of the ingredients, not including the potatoes and quinoa. Lock lid and let cook for 30 minutes on High. Quick release pressure when time is up.
2. Then add in the potatoes and quinoa and cook on High for another 10 minutes. Quick release when time is up. Stir in the cilantro and serve hot.

Hearty Beef Cabbage Soup

Serving: 8

Total time taken: 30 min

Ingredients:

- 1 pound ground beef
- 1 teaspoon kosher salt
- ½ cup diced onion
- ½ cup diced celery
- ½ cup diced carrot
- 4 large tomatoes, diced
- 5 cups chopped green cabbage
- 6 cups beef stock
- Black pepper to taste
- 2 bay leaves

Directions:

1. On Sauté add in beef and a drizzle of olive oil and sauté until golden brown.
2. Add in the beef stock and the rest of the ingredients, lock the lid cook High pressure for 20 minutes.
3. Once time is up let the steam release naturally. Remove bay leaves and serve. Season to your liking.

Broccoli Cheddar Cheese Soup

Serving: 4

Total time taken: 15

Ingredients:

- 1 pound fresh broccoli, chopped
- 2 cups shredded cheddar cheese
- 1 small onion chopped
- 4 cups chicken broth
- 2 cups heavy cream
- 1 cup shredded carrots
- 2 tablespoon hot sauce
- Salt to taste

Directions:

1. Place chopped onion, carrots, broccoli, and chicken broth in the Pressure Cooker and cook on High pressure for 15 minutes. When time is up, quick release and stir in heavy cream.
2. Place pot back on sauté until comes to a low boil about 5 minutes. Stir in cheese and hot sauce. Stir until cheese is melted.
3. Serve with bread or crackers and sa t and pepper to taste.

Rustic Vegetable Soup

Serving: 6

Total time taken: 20 min

Ingredients:

- 2 large russet potatoes, peeled and cut into cubes
- 1 carrot, diced
- 2 cups corn tidbits
- 1 cup rinsed drained canned fava beans
- 1 cup frozen peas
- 1 teaspoon ground cumin
- 6 cups vegetable broth
- Kosher salt and freshly ground black pepper
- ¼ cup chopped fresh cilantro
- 1 avocado, peeled and cut into 6 wedges, for garnish

Directions:

1. In the inner pot, combine potatoes, carrot, corn, fava beans, peas, cumin and broth.
2. Lock the lid and cook on High Pressure. Use the button to decrease the time on the display to 20 minutes. When time is up, release pressure naturally.
3. Stir well and season to taste with salt and pepper. Ladle into serving bowls, garnish with cilantro and top each with 1 avocado wedge.

Creamy Pumpkin Corn Soup

Serving: 4

Total time taken: 20 min

Ingredients:

- 2 tablespoons butter
- 1 cup diced onion
- 1 garlic clove, minced
- 6 cups chicken broth
- 2 cups canned Pumpkin Puree
- 1 teaspoon dried parsley flakes
- ¼ teaspoon freshly ground black pepper
- ¼ teaspoon dried red pepper flakes
- ¼ teaspoon freshly grated nutmeg
- 2 large russet potatoes, cubed
- 2 large boneless skinless chicken breasts, diced into bite sized cubes
- 2 cups frozen corn
- ½ cup heavy cream

Directions:

1. Add butter to the pressure cooking pot. When butter is melted, add the onion and cook, stirring until the onion is tender, about 5 minutes. Add garlic and cook 1 minute.
2. Add chicken broth, pumpkin puree, Italian seasoning, pepper, red pepper flakes, and nutmeg to the pressure cooking pot. Stir to combine.
3. Add the diced potatoes and diced chicken. Lock lid in place, select High Pressure and 4 minutes cook time and start. When timer beeps, do quick pressure release. Stir in corn and

heavy cream. Add salt and pepper to taste. Bring back to a simmer on sauté mode for another 5 minutes, then serve topped with chopped parsley.

VEGETABLES	ELECTRIC PRESSURE COOKER (10-12PSI)	STOVETOP PRESSURE COOKER (13-15PSI)	PRESSURE SELECTION	OPENING METHOD
Artichoke, hearts	3	3	High or Low	Normal
Artichoke, pieces or baby	4	4	High or Low	Normal
Artichoke, whole (small, med, large)	5, 8, 11	5, 8, 11	High or Low	Normal
Asparagus	1	1	High or Low	Normal
Beans (see BEANS & LEGUMES)				
Beet, Cubed	4	4	High or Low	
Beet, Greens	2	2		Normal
Beet, Whole (small, med, large)	10, 15, 20	8, 10, 15	High	Normal
Bok Choy, baby	1	1	High or Low	Normal
Bok Choy	5 to 7	5 to 7	High or Low	Normal
Broccoli	3 to 5	3 to 5	High or Low	Normal
Brussels Sprouts	4	4	High or Low	Normal
Cabbage, Red, Green, Savoy	3	3	High or Low	Normal
Capsicums (see Peppers)				
Carrots, sliced	1 to 2	1 to 2	High or Low	Normal
Carrots, whole	3 to 4	3 to 4	High or Low	Normal
Cauliflower, florets	2 to 3	2 to 3	High or Low	Normal
Cauliflower, whole	10	8	High or Low	Normal
Celeriac	3 to 4	3 to 4	High or Low	Normal
Celery, sliced	2 to 3	2 to 3	High or Low	Normal
Chard, swiss	2	2	High or Low	Normal
Chicory	5 to 7	5 to 7	High or Low	Normal
Chinese Cabbage (see Bok Choy)				
Collards	3 to 4	3 to 4	High or Low	Normal
Corn, kernels	1	1	High or Low	Normal

Cream of Zucchini Soup

Serving: 5

Total time taken: 30 min

Ingredients:

- 1 pound zucchini, washed and cut into chunks
- 1 large potato, diced
- 2 cloves garlic, minced
- 1 handful chopped fresh coriander
- 1 small onion, roughly chopped
- Salt and pepper to taste
- 5 cups vegetable stock
- 1 cup heavy cream

Directions:

1. Put all the ingredients except the cream, inside inner pot and select Soup and let it cook for 20 minutes. Lock lid.
2. Once time is up naturally release pressure, and stir in the heavy cream and let it cool then blend everything in a blender until smooth. Add it back to the inner pot and bring it to a boil. Adjust seasoning to your liking.
3. Serve with fresh bread and crackers.

Winter Vegetable Soup

Serving: 6

Total time taken: 45 min

Ingredients:

- 2 cups chopped carrots
- 2 large potatoes peeled and chopped
- 2 large onions, chopped
- 2 large tomatoes diced
- 1 purple yam, diced
- 1 cup corn tidbits
- ½ cup sundried tomatoes
- ¼ cup quinoa rinsed
- 1 tablespoon dried basil
- 1 tablespoon garlic minced
- 1 tablespoon hot sauce
- ½ tablespoon dried oregano
- 1 teaspoon onion powder
- ½ teaspoon salt
- ¼ teaspoon ground black pepper
- 6 cups vegetable stock

Directions:

1. Add all ingredients to the Pressure Cooker and lock lid.
2. Cook on High Pressure and set the time to 20 minutes. When time is up use quick release.

3. Give the soup a quick stir and adjust seasoning to your liking. Serve with warm dinner rolls and butter.

VEGETABLES	ELECTRIC PRESSURE COOKER (10-12PSI)	STOVETOP PRESSURE COOKER (13-15PSI)	PRESSURE SELECTION	OPENING METHOD
Artichoke, hearts	3	3	High or Low	Normal
Artichoke, pieces or baby	4	4	High or Low	Normal
Artichoke, whole (small, med, large)	5, 8, 11	5, 8, 11	High or Low	Normal
Asparagus	1	1	High or Low	Normal
Beans (see BEANS & LEGUMES)				
Beet, Cubed	4	4	High or Low	
Beet, Greens	2	2		Normal
Beet, Whole (small, med, large)	10, 15, 20	8, 10, 15	High	Normal
Bok Choy, baby	1	1	High or Low	Normal
Bok Choy	5 to 7	5 to 7	High or Low	Normal
Broccoli	3 to 5	3 to 5	High or Low	Normal
Brussels Sprouts	4	4	High or Low	Normal
Cabbage, Red, Green, Savoy	3	3	High or Low	Normal
Capsicums (see Peppers)				
Carrots, sliced	1 to 2	1 to 2	High or Low	Normal
Carrots, whole	3 to 4	3 to 4	High or Low	Normal
Cauliflower, florets	2 to 3	2 to 3	High or Low	Normal
Cauliflower, whole	10	8	High or Low	Normal
Celeriac	3 to 4	3 to 4	High or Low	Normal
Celery, sliced	2 to 3	2 to 3	High or Low	Normal
Chard, swiss	2	2	High or Low	Normal
Chicory	5 to 7	5 to 7	High or Low	Normal
Chinese Cabbage (see Bok Choy)				
Collards	3 to 4	3 to 4	High or Low	Normal
Corn, kernels	1	1	High or Low	Normal

Meatball and Vegetable Soup

Serving: 8

Total time taken: 20

Ingredients:

Meatballs

- 1 pound ground beef
- ¼ cup fresh cilantro, chopped
- ¼ cup fresh dill, chopped
- 1 teaspoon sea salt
- 1 egg beaten
- 1 yellow onion, finely chopped

Vegetable Soup

- 1 cup peas
- 1 cup corn tidbits
- 2 large carrots, chopped
- 6 cups beef stock
- ¼ cup cooked Jasmine rice
- Salt and pepper to taste

Directions:

1. In a large mixing bowl, combine the meatball ingredients and roll out meatballs, roughly size of golf balls and set them aside on a plate

2. On Sauté mode, bring to a boil the beef stock, stir in the peas, corn and carrots. Then place your meatballs into the stock. Lock lid and press Soup, decrease time to 15 minutes. Once time is up do quick release.
3. Add in the rice and press Soup and decrease time to 15 minutes. Once time is up let naturally release pressure, adjust seasoning to your liking. Serve immediately and top with freshly chopped cilantro.

Add Your Own Tips & Tricks

Lemon Garlic Lamb Stew

Serving: 4

Total time taken: 1 hour

Ingredients:

- 1 pound lamb cubed
- 1 teaspoon salt
- 2 tablespoons olive oil
- 1 shallot finely chopped
- 3 gloves garlic minced
- Juice of 1 lemon
- 1 cup red wine
- 5 cups beef stock
- 1 sprig fresh rosemary 6 to 8 inches long
- 2 bay leaves
- 1 tablespoon oregano
- 2 cups mushrooms quartered
- 4 carrots, cubed
- 1 bunch roughly chopped parsley leaves

Directions:

1. On Sauté mode, add olive oil and sauté lamb with garlic, salt and shallot for 5 minutes.
2. Then add in the red wine, beef stock and oregano. Bring to a simmer, stir for 5 minutes.
3. Add in the rest of the ingredients and lock lid and press Soup.
4. Decrease time to 40 minutes.
5. Once time is up, let it release pressure naturally.

6. Stir in the lemon juice and adjust seasoning to your liking.
7. Ladle stew into bowls, and garnish with chopped parsley. Serve with crusty bread.

MEAT POULTRY & DARY	ELECTRIC PRESSURE COOKER (10-12PSI)	STOVETOP PRESSURE COOKER (13-15PSI)	FROZEN*	PRESSURE SELECTION	OPENING METHOD
Beef, brisket	70	50	no	High	Natural
Beef, flank steak	15	10	+ 10	High	Normal, Natural
Beef, ground	6	6	+4	High	Natural
Beef, Osso buco	25	20	+ 10-15	High	Natural
Beef, ox tail	45	30	+15	High	Natural
Beef, ribs	60	45	+10	High	Natural
Beef, roast	75	60	no	High	Natural
Beef, round	60	50	no	High	Natural
Beef, stew (cubed)	12	10	+5		Normal, Natural
Beef, stock (bones, ect.)	60	45	+15	High	Natural
Beef, tongue	50	40	no	High	Natural
Boar, roast	45	30	no	High	Natural
Boar, stew (cubed)	20	15	+10	High	Normal, Natural
Cheese	see instructions			High	Natural
Chicken, breast boneless & skinless (boil, steam)	1, 6	1, 4	+4	High	Natural
Chicken, ground	5	4	+4	High	Natural
Chicken, liver	3	3	+4	High	Normal
Chicken, bone-in pieces (leg, thigh, breast, wings)	10	8	+ 5-7	High	Natural
Chicken, stock (bones, ect.)	35	30	+10	High	Natural
Chicken, strips	1	1	+4	High	Natural

German Style Sausage Stew

Serving: 4

Total time taken: 15-25

Ingredients:

- 1 pound of kielbasa, or your favorite sausage meat, cut into medium to large pieces
- 2 large russet potatoes, quartered
- 1 can (14 oz.) diced tomatoes
- 1 small jar sauerkraut
- 1 onion cut into large chunks

Directions:

1. Add all ingredients to the pot.
2. Press Soup button and adjust time to 20 minutes.
3. After the time is up do quick release. Give everything a good stir. Serve with warm crusty bread.

Pressure Cooker Seafood Chowder

Serving: 6

Total time taken: 35 min

Ingredients:

- 2 pounds fresh cod, cut into thick strips
- 1 pound baby shrimp, rinsed, drained
- ½ pound clam meat, rinsed, drained
- 2 tablespoon butter
- 1 onion, chopped
- 1 cup sliced mushrooms
- 4 medium sized potatoes, peeled, diced
- 4 cups fish stock
- 1 teaspoon Old Bay Seasoning (or more)
- Salt & Pepper to taste
- 1 cup clam juice
- ½ cup white wine
- 1 cup heavy cream

Directions:

1. In Sauté mode, add the onions and sauté until soft with a little bit of olive oil. About 2 minutes.
2. Add in the fish stock, clam juice and white wine into inner pot and bring to a boil. Then add in the seafood and seasoning, potatoes and mushrooms. Lock lid and press Soup and decrease time to 20 minutes. Lock lid.

3. Once time is up, naturally release pressure and stir in the heavy cream, and adjust seasoning to taste. Serve with fresh dinner rolls.

SEAFOOD	ELECTRIC PRESSURE COOKER (10-12PSI)	STOVETOP PRESSURE COOKER (13-15PSI)	PRESSURE SELECTION	OPENING METHOD
Calamari	20	15 to 18	High	Normal
Carp	6	4	High	Normal
Clams, canned/jarred	add after pressure cooking			Normal
Clams, fresh	6	4	High	Normal
Cod	3	3	Low	Normal
Crab	3	2	Low	Normal
Eel	10	8	High	Normal
Fish fillet	3	2	Low	Normal
Fish soup or stock	6	5	High	Normal
Fish steak	4	3	High	Normal
Fish, mixed pieces (for fish soup)	8	6	Low	Normal
Fish, whole, gutted	6	5	Low	Normal
Fish, in packet (Al Cartoccio)	15	12	High	Normal
Frog's Legs	8	8	High	Normal
Haddock	7	6	Low	Normal
Halibut	7	6	Low	Normal
Lobster	12	8	Low	Normal
Lobster, 2 lb (1k)	3	2	Low	Normal
Mussels	1	1	Low	Normal
Ocean Perch	7	6	Low	Normal
Octopus	20	15	High	Normal, Natural
Oysters	6	4	Low	Normal
Perch	6	4	Low	Normal
Prawns (see Shrimp)				
Salmon	6	5	Low	Normal

Easy Sunday Chili

Serving: 8

Total time taken: 35 min

Ingredients:

- 1 pound lean ground beef
- 1 teaspoon olive oil
- 2 cloves minced garlic
- 1 large onion, chopped
- 1 large bell pepper, chopped
- 4 stalks celery, chopped
- 1 beef broth
- 1 (15 oz.) can dark red kidney beans, drained
- 1 (15 oz.) can diced tomatoes
- 1 (15 oz.) can tomato sauce
- Salt and pepper to taste
- 2 cups shredded cheddar cheese

Directions:

1. Set your Pressure Cooker to Sauté and add olive oil and minced garlic to the pot sauté for 1 minute then add your beef and brown it for another 5 minutes.
2. Add in the beef broth and bring to boil. Once boiling add in rest of ingredients and select Meat/Stew and default time to 35 minutes. Once time is up, do quick release pressure.
3. Give it a good stir then serve with cheddar cheese.

Easy Sunday Vegan Chili

Serving: 6

Total time taken: 30 min

Ingredients:

- 1 can (19 oz.) black bean soup
- 1 can (15 oz.) kidney beans, drained
- 1 small white onion, chopped
- 1 large poblano pepper, chopped
- 2 large red peppers, diced
- 2 large tomatoes, diced
- 1 jalapeno, diced
- 1 teaspoon chili powder
- 2 teaspoon cumin
- 1 teaspoon paprika
- 1 teaspoon sea salt
- ¼ tsp cayenne pepper
- 1 sweet potato, peeled and chopped into small chunks
- 1 cup corn tidbits
- ½ cup beer (pilsner or lager)

Directions:

1. Add all the ingredients into Pressure Cooker and mix well. Lock lid and select Chili button and default time to 30 minutes.
2. When time is up, let it naturally release pressure. Give everything a stir and adjust seasoning to your liking. Serve with tortilla chips on the side and fresh lemon wedges.

Pressure Cooker Appetizers Recipes

BBQ Sauce Chicken Drumsticks

Serving: 8

Total time taken: 25-30

Ingredients:

- 10 medium sized chicken drumsticks
- 2 cloves minced garlic
- 1 cup barbecue sauce
- ¼ cup sweet paprika
- 4 teaspoons freshly ground black pepper
- 1 ½ teaspoons cayenne pepper
- 1 ½ teaspoons garlic powder
- 1 ½ teaspoons dry mustard
- 1 ½ teaspoons ground cumin

Directions:

1. In large mixing bowl, marinate chicken drumsticks with all the seasoning and barbecue sauce. Add it to your Pressure Cooker and drizzle about 1 cup of chicken broth over the drumsticks.
2. Lock lid and press Poultry, change cook time to 25 minutes.
3. Once time is up release pressure naturally and serve immediately with your favorite sides.

Honey Teriyaki Chicken Wings

Serving: 4

Total time taken: 25 min

Ingredients:

- 2 pounds chicken wings
- 1 cup chicken stock
- 1 cup soy sauce
- ½ cup rice wine
- 1 cup honey
- 2 cloves minced garlic
- 1 teaspoon fresh grated ginger
- 1 teaspoon sriracha
- Chopped scallions

Directions:

1. On Sauté mode, quickly sauté the wings with the minced garlic. Add a drizzle of olive oil. Sauté until most of the wings are browned 10 to 15 minutes.
2. Add in the rest of the ingredients, except for the chopped scallions. Cook on High pressure for 20 minutes. Once time is up naturally release pressure.
3. Sprinkle fresh scallions and serve.

Pressure Cooker Chicken Paprika

Serving: 4

Total time taken: 15

Ingredients:

- 4 medium sized chicken breasts
- 1 tablespoon olive oil
- 1 teaspoon salt
- 1 cup chicken stock
- 3 tablespoons paprika powder
- 2 large cloves of garlic, finely diced
- 1 tablespoon tomato paste
- 2 heaped tablespoons sour cream

Directions:

1. In large mixing bowl season each chicken breasts with salt, paprika and tomato paste.
2. Select Sauté and quickly sauté garlic with olive oil for about a minute then using tongs brown each side of the chicken breasts. Leave the breasts in the Pressure Cooker then add in the chicken stock.
3. Lock lid and cook on High pressure for 15 minutes. Once time is up let it release pressure naturally.
4. Serve with fresh cracked pepper and sea salt over a green salad and a dollop of the sour cream on each cooked breast.

Sweet and Spicy Meatballs

Serving: 4

Total time taken: 35

Ingredients:

- 1 pound ground beef
- ¼ cup bread crumbs
- 1 egg, beaten
- 2 tablespoons water
- 2 tablespoons ketchup
- Salt and pepper, to taste
- 1 cup marinara sauce
- 1 cup apple jelly
- 2 tablespoon hot chili oil

Directions:

1. Mix chopped meat thoroughly with bread crumbs, egg, water, ketchup, salt and pepper. Shape into balls and place in bottom of Pressure Cooker.
2. Mix together marinara sauce, apple jelly and hot chili oil and pour over meatballs.
3. Press Meat/Stew and default time to 35 minutes. Once time is up do quick release pressure Serve with your favorite pasta or rice.

Barbecue Pork Ribs

Serving: 4

Total time taken: 35-40 min

Ingredients:

- 2 racks of pork ribs
- 3 cups barbeque sauce
- 1 cup beef broth
- 2 yellow onions, diced
- 3 gloves minced garlic
- 1 tablespoon chili powder

Directions:

1. Season ribs generously with salt and pepper and the chili powder.
2. Place ribs into Pressure Cooker and pour the barbeque sauce and beef broth over ribs and then sprinkle the onions and minced garlic over ribs.
3. Lick lid and press Meat and adjust time to 35 minutes. Once time is up, release pressure naturally and serve immediately with fresh salad.

BBQ Smoked Sausage

Serving: 10

Total time taken: 25 min

Ingredients:

- 2 pounds smoked breakfast sausage, sliced in half
- 2 cups Jack Daniel's honey Smokehouse barbecue sauce
- ½ tablespoon brown sugar
- ½ tablespoon lemon juice
- 1-2 cups beef stock

Directions:

1. Add all ingredients into Pressure Cooker and submerge ingredients with 1-2 cups of beef stock.
2. Lock lid and cook on High Pressure for 25 minutes.
3. Once time is up do quick release and serve with crackers and crusty bread.

Chinese Boiled Peanuts

Serving: 4

Total time taken: 1 hour 25 min

Ingredients:

- 1 pound Jumbo Raw Peanuts
- 3 Star Anise
- 3 Cinnamon Sticks
- 3 Cloves Fresh Garlic
- 3 Tablespoons Kosher Salt
- 1 chunk Rock Sugar optional
- 4 Dried Red Chili Peppers

Directions:

1. Rinse peanuts under cool water and remove any twigs, roots, whatever doesn't belong.
2. Add peanuts and all ingredients to your Pressure Cooker cooking pot and cover with water. Place a plate or trivet on top to hold down the peanuts.
3. Lock on lid and close Pressure Valve.
4. Cook on High Pressure for 60-80 minutes.
5. When Beep is heard, allow all pressure to release naturally and let sit 30 minutes.

Sweet and Sour Meatballs

Serving: 4

Total time taken: 35-40 min

Ingredients:

- 1 bag frozen fully cooked beef meatballs
- ½ cups rice vinegar
- ½ cups Ketchup
- ½ cups honey
- 2 cups chunk pineapple, canned, drained
- 2 tablespoons Soy Sauce
- 1 cup dice Bell Pepper, Red
- 1 cup dice Bell Pepper, Green

Directions:

1. Mix together rice vinegar, ketchup, brown sugar, pineapple and juice, and soy sauce.
2. Place meatballs and sauce in the inner pot, and the peppers and pineapple. Press Meat/Stew and default time to 35 minutes. Once time is up release pressure naturally.
3. Serve with cucumber sticks and celery sticks.

Corn on the Cob

Serving: 6

Total time taken: 8 min

Ingredients:

- 6 ears of corn
- Butter for serving
- Lemon Pepper salt seasoning for serving

Directions:

1. Lay inside the pot rack. You may have to break some ears in half. Stagger them to allow steam to pass through. Add 1 cup of water. Point the steam release to SEALING
2. Press the Manual button for 8 minutes. Use quick release. That's all you do. The corn never touches the water.

The Ultimate Loaded Potato Skins

Serving: 4

Total time taken: 30 min

Ingredients:

- 1 pound bacon, cut into chunks
- 1 cup water
- 6 medium russet potatoes
- 2 tablespoon melted butter
- 2 cups shredded cheddar
- 1 cup sour cream
- Fresh chives for garnish

Directions:

1. Preheat the pressure cooker on sauté. Cook the bacon in the pot until browned. Remove the inner pot and drain the bacon and grease onto paper towels.
2. Pour a small amount of water in and use the sauté selection to deglaze the pot. Pour 1 cup of water in.
3. Place the potatoes in an ovenproof (7 inch diameter) strainer and lower into the pot with the trivet.
4. Place the lid on and locked. Press the manual button and adjust the time to 12 minutes. Once time is up release pressure naturally. Take the potatoes out and allow them to cool enough to handle. Slice the potatoes in half and scoop out the center of each half. Save the scooped potatoes for another use.
5. Brush the bottom of each potato with melted butter and place on a baking sheet. Distribute the cheese evenly over each potato half. Top each with bacon.

6. Place the baking sheet under the broiler on the center rack in the oven. Broil on high for 2 to 3 minutes, or until the cheese is melted. Remove from oven and top each potato with sour cream and chives.

Add Your Own Tips & Tricks

Eggplant Caponatina

Serving: 4

Total time taken: 25 min

Ingredients:

- 1 large Eggplant, cubed
- 1 teaspoon salt
- ¼ cup olive oil
- 2 medium Zucchini, cut into rounds
- 1 onion, cut into thin wedges
- 2 medium potatoes, cubed
- 10 cherry tomatoes, halved
- 1 tablespoon Capers
- 2 tablespoons pine nuts
- 1 tablespoons raisins
- ¼ cup olives, pits removed
- 1 bunch basil, chopped
- Salt and Pepper to taste

Directions:

1. Season eggplant with salt. Select Sauté mode on your Pressure Cooker and sauté eggplant for 5 minutes.
2. Add the rest of the ingredients and sauté for another minute. Drizzle about ½ cup of water salt and pepper over everything.
3. Lock lid and press Steam and default time to 10 minutes. When time is up use quick release. Give everything a stir and serve over rice or rice crackers.

Crispy Roasted Yukon Potatoes

Serving: 4

Total time taken: 30 min

Ingredients:

- 5 tablespoon olive oil
- 1 ½ pounds baby Yukon potatoes
- Kosher salt, ground pepper, garlic salt to taste
- 2 Rosemary sprigs
- ½ cup water

Directions:

1. Pour water into Pressure Cooker and place steamer basket in and add your potatoes and rosemary sprigs.
2. Lock lid and select Steam and default time to 10 minutes. One time is up do quick release pressure. Place the potatoes on a baking sheet, brush with olive oil and sprinkle seasoning.
3. Broil in middle rack for 15 minutes. Serve immediately.

Easy Hummus Dip

Serving: 10

Total time taken: 1 hour

Ingredients:

- 1 pound dried chickpeas, rinsed
- 6 cups water
- 3 cups chickpeas
- 2 medium cloves garlic
- Juice from 1 large lemon
- 1 teaspoons kosher salt
- ½ teaspoon ground cumin
- ¼ teaspoon smoked paprika
- ¼ cup high quality extra virgin olive oil

Directions:

1. Add all the ingredients to your Pressure Cooker and select Steam button and adjust time to 20 minutes. Lock lid and let it cook. Once time is up do quick release pressure.
2. Ladle everything into a blender and blend until smooth.
3. Transfer to serving bowl and drizzle more olive oil and a sprinkle of cumin powder of the hummus. Serve with pita bread and fresh vegetables.

Thai Baked Sweet Potatoes

Serving: 4

Total time taken: 20 min

Ingredients:

- 1 cup water
- 4 medium sweet potatoes
- 2 medium sweet potatoes
- ¼ teaspoon Thai Red Curry Paste
- 1 teaspoon freshly grated ginger
- 5 tablespoon unsweetened Coconut Milk

Directions:

1. Place steamer basket in Pressure Cooker and add 1 cup water. Scrub sweet potatoes until skins are clean. Place on top of the steamer basket.
2. Cover and place vent on lid to Sealed. Set on Steam and set time for 10 minutes.
3. When finished cooking, don't open lid. Allow pressure to reduce naturally, about 25 minutes.
4. Cut the potatoes lengthwise and scoop out the orange flesh, keeping the skins intact. Place flesh into a mixing bowl with remaining ingredients. Blend until smooth. Place potato skin halves in a baking dish. Distribute sweet potato mixture among the skins. Bake uncovered for 10 minutes. Garnish with chives.

Ginger Honey Glazed Carrots

Serving: 4

Total time taken: 10 min

Ingredients:

- 3 pounds carrots, cleaned and trimmed
- 1 tablespoon butter
- 1 teaspoon ginger powder
- 1 teaspoon sesame seeds
- 1 tablespoon honey

Directions:

1. Place your Pressure Cooker on high sauté and add butter. Let it melt and add in your carrots. Sauté for just a minute or two. Add in the ginger powder, and honey.
2. Put on and lock lid in place with Pressure Cooker on manual for 4 minutes. Once it has come to pressure and time is up, quick release the steam using an oven mitt. Remove from Pressure Cooker, sprinkle sesame seeds and serve.

Garlic Mashed Potatoes

Serving: 4

Total time taken: 25 min

Ingredients:

- 4 russet potatoes
- 1 cup water
- 100 ml milk
- 2 tablespoons unsalted butter
- 2 cloves garlic, minced
- 2 tablespoons grated Parmesan cheese
- Kosher salt and pepper to taste

Directions:

1. Fill the pressure cooker with 1 cup of water. Place the steamer trivet in the pot and add quartered potatoes in the steamer trivet. Close the lid. Cook in High Pressure for 8 minutes, then quick release.
2. While the potatoes are cooking, heat a small sauce pan over medium heat. Melt the butter and add the garlic. Add a pinch of kosher salt. Sauté the garlic for 1 to 2 minutes until fragrant and golden in color. Add the milk and deglaze the pan. Remove mixture from heat when it is hot.
3. Remove the lid. Mash the cooked potatoes in a medium mixing bowl with a potato masher. Add half of the garlic butter mixture to the bowl. Continue to mash, stir, and add the mixture until desired consistency. Taste and season with salt and pepper. Serve warm.

Wild Mushroom Risotto

Serving: 6

Total time taken: 20 min

Ingredients:

- 4 ounces Dried Porcini
- 2 cups fresh Cremini Mushrooms roughly chopped
- 1 tablespoon butter
- 1 tablespoon olive oil
- 1 ½ cups Arborio Rice
- 3 chopped large shallots
- ½ cup dry white wine
- 2 cups chicken stock
- ½ teaspoon Sea Salt
- 1 cup Parmesan
- 2 tablespoons fresh chopped parsley leaves

Directions:

1. Add all ingredients into Pressure Cooker, not including the Parmesan and parsley leaves.
2. Select Rice and default time to 20 minutes. Once time is up, do quick release pressure.
3. Mix in the Parmesan and parsley leaves and serve immediately.

Root Vegetable Medley

Serving: 6

Total time taken: 1 hour

Ingredients:

- 3 beets, peeled, cubed
- 2 carrots, cubed
- 2 turnips, cubed
- 1 large onion, chopped
- 1 large parsnips, chopped
- 1 cup water
- 1 tablespoon butter
- Fresh thyme, parsley, or rosemary sprigs for garnish
- 1 teaspoon whole cumin

Directions:

1. Turn on Pressure Cooker and select Sauté and add oil and cumin, once it starts crackling add in the onion and sauté until tender.
2. Add the rest of the root vegetables and water. Press Steam and let it steam for 15 minutes. Once time is up let it naturally release pressure.
3. Serve with your favorite dip.

Pressure Cooker Meat Poultry Recipes

Spicy Honey Garlic Chicken

Serving: 4

Total time taken: 15 min

Ingredients:

- 3 pounds boneless, skinless chicken drumsticks
- 1/2 teaspoon dried minced garlic
- 1 teaspoons Sriracha chili garlic sauce
- 3/4 cup soy sauce
- 3/4 cup ketchup
- 3/4 cup honey
- 2 tablespoons cornstarch
- 2 tablespoons water
- 1 tablespoon chopped fresh basil

Directions:

1. Add garlic, chili sauce, soy sauce, ketchup and honey to pressure cooking pot. Stir to combine. Add chicken to the pot. Cover pot and lock lid in place.
2. Select High Pressure and 9 minutes cook time.
3. After 9 minutes cook time, turn off pressure cooker and use a quick pressure release.
4. In a small bowl, dissolve cornstarch in 2 tablespoons water. Add cornstarch mixture to the sauce in the pot stirring constantly. Select Simmer and bring to a boil, stirring constantly. After sauce thickens, add fresh basil to the sauce.

Pressure Cooker Roast Chicken

Serving: 4

Total time taken: 60 min

Ingredients:

- One small chicken – about 4 pounds
- 1 tablespoon coconut oil
- 1 cup baby carrots
- 1 stalk celery, chopped
- 1 medium onion, chopped
- 4 cloves garlic, peeled
- Juice of 1 lemon
- Sea salt and pepper for seasoning
- 1 sprig of rosemary
- 1 cup chicken stock

Directions:

1. First rub the chicken with the coconut oil, then stuff the carrots, celery and garlic inside the crevice of the chicken. Use twine to secure the legs together.
2. Place chicken inside inner pot and then add in couple cracks of sea salt and pepper over the breast. Drizzle the lemon juice and chicken stock over the chicken.
3. Place the chopped onion around the chicken and lock lid. Select Poultry and default time to 25 minutes. Once timer is up. Quick release pressure and place the sprig of rosemary on top of the chicken.
4. Lock lid again and cook on High Pressure for another 20 minutes. Naturally release pressure. Careful when removing the chicken. Serve with favorite sides.

Meat	Cooking Time (in Minutes)
Beef, stew meat	15 – 20
Beef, meat ball	10 -15
Beef, dressed	20 – 25
Beef, pot roast, steak, rump, round, chuck, blade or brisket, large	35 – 40
Beef, pot roast, steak, rump, round, chuck, blade or brisket, small chunks	25 – 30
Beef, ribs	25 – 30
Beef, shanks	25 – 30
Beef, oxtail	40 – 50
Chicken, breasts	8 – 10
Chicken, whole	20 – 25
Chicken, cut up with bones	10 – 15
Chicken, drumsticks, legs or thighs	10 – 15
Cornish Hen, whole	10 – 15
Duck, cut up with bones	10 – 12
Duck, whole	25 – 30
Ham slice	9 – 12
Ham picnic shoulder	25 – 30
Lamb, cubes,	10 -15
Lamb, stew meat	10 -15
Lamb, leg	35 – 45
Pheasant	20 – 25
Pork, loin roast	55 – 60
Pork, butt roast	45 – 50
Pork, ribs	20 – 25
Turkey, breast, boneless	15 – 20
Turkey, breast, whole, with bones	25 – 30
Turkey, drumsticks (leg)	15 – 20
Veal, chops	5 – 8
Veal, roast	35 – 45
Quail, whole	8 – 10

Open Chicken Pot Pie

Serving: 6

Total time taken: 35 min

Ingredients:

- 2 pounds chicken breasts cut into 2-inch pieces
- 1 small onion, diced
- 1 pound mixed frozen vegetables
- 3 cups Chicken Stock
- 3 medium Potatoes peeled & chunked
- 1 teaspoon Herbs de Provence
- 1 teaspoon seasoning salt
- 1 can Cream of Chicken Soup
- ½ cup Water
- 1 teaspoons Herbs de Provence
- ¼ teaspoon Freshly Ground Black Pepper

Directions:

1. Add all the ingredients not including the chicken and potatoes, into inner pot, bring to boil on Sauté mode. Once boiling give everything a stir, place cut chicken breasts on top of the ingredients, lock lid and press Soup, default time to 20 minutes.
2. Once time is up, quick release, then add in the potatoes and cock on High for another 15 minutes. Once time is up let it naturally release pressure.
3. Stir well, adjust seasoning and serve with warm dinner rolls.

Chicken and Pancetta Risotto

Serving: 4

Total time taken: 20 min

Ingredients:

- 1 onion, chopped
- 2 garlic cloves, chopped
- 2 teaspoon sesame oil
- Freshly ground black pepper
- ½ cup pancetta, diced
- ½ cup diced chicken
- 2 cups Arborio rice
- 1 cup grated parmesan
- 1 cup Small glass white wine
- 1 cup chicken stock
- 1 teaspoon dried thyme
- Grated zest of 1 lemon
- Basil leaves for garnish

Directions:

1. Press Sauté to preheat the Pressure Cooker, add the oil to the pan. Sauté the onion, garlic, pancetta and chicken for about 2 minutes.
2. Stir in the rice, season well, add the thyme, and stir in the wine. Pour in the stock and stir really well.
3. Cook on High pressure for 12 minutes. Once time is up naturally release pressure.

4. At the end of the cooking time, stir the risotto well to develop the creamy texture, and stir in the grated parmesan, and leave to stand for 3 minutes.
5. Serve topped with extra parmesan, freshly ground black pepper, and grated lemon zest and basil leaves.

Sunday Night Chicken Dinner

Serving: 4

Total time taken: 25

Ingredients:

- 2 pounds boneless chicken breasts
- ½ pound fresh green beans, ends trimmed
- 1 ½ pounds diced red potatoes
- ⅓ cup fresh lemon juice
- ¼ cup olive oil
- 1 teaspoon dried oregano
- 1 teaspoon salt
- ¼ teaspoon pepper
- ¼ teaspoon onion powder
- 2 garlic cloves, minced

Directions:

1. Start by placing the chicken in a 6-quart slow cooker, in the center. Next add the green beans on one side. Then for the potatoes.
2. In a medium sized bowl, whisk together the lemon juice, olive oil, oregano, salt, pepper, onion powder and garlic cloves.

3. Pour this mixture evenly over the chicken, green beans and potatoes.
4. Cover and cook on High pressure for 35 minutes. Once time is up let it naturally release pressure. Serve immediately.

Add Your Own Tips & Tricks

Pressure Cooker Osos Bunco

Serving: 4

Total time taken: 2 hr. 30 min

Ingredients:

- 4 veal or lamb shanks that will fit inside inner pot
- ¼ cup flour
- ½ teaspoon black pepper
- ½ teaspoon salt
- ½ teaspoon garlic powder
- ½ teaspoon onion powder
- 1 teaspoon thyme
- 1 teaspoon rosemary
- ¼ cup olive oil
- 1 tablespoon butter
- 2 medium carrots chopped in large chunks
- 2 stalks celery cut into large chunks
- 1 medium onion chopped
- 2 cloves crushed garlic
- 2 cups chicken broth
- 2 pounds red potatoes
- 1 tablespoon butter

Directions:

1. Add the flour and the seasonings to a large bowl. Use a wire whsk to blend everything together. Rinse the shanks and dry with a paper towel. Roll each shank in the flour mix and set

aside on a plate (Keep the remaining flour). Preheat a large skillet. Add the oil and bring to almost smoking. Place the shanks in the skillet and brown turning each shank to brown all sides of the shank. Once they are browned, set aside. Add the flour to the remaining oil and make a rue. Once the rue is made add the broth to loosen the rue into a sauce.

2. Pour ½ of the sauce inside inner pot and place each shank into the sauce and fill in the gaps with the vegetables. Pour the remaining sauce over the shanks and vegetables. Lock lid and press Slow Cook and default time to 2 hours. Once time is up use natural release.

3. Towards the end of the cooking cycle, boil the red potatoes (skin on) until tender. Mash the potatoes adding 1 tablespoon of butter. Salt and pepper to taste.

4. Serve a lamb shank on a bed of potatoes. Add a large spoon of the vegetables. Ladle on some of the sauce from the cooker over the shank, vegetables and potatoes.

Roast Turkey Breast and Gravy

Serving: 8

Total time taken: 50 min

Ingredients:

- 2 pounds turkey breasts
- 1 teaspoon of each salt, pepper, garlic powder, onion powder, and paprika
- 1 (14 oz.) can chicken broth
- 1 large onion, quartered
- 1 stock celery, cut in large pieces
- 1 sprig of thyme
- 3 cloves of garlic
- 3 tablespoons cornstarch
- 3 tablespoons cold water

Directions:

1. Put a slice into the turkey breasts to create a pocket. Season turkey breast liberally with spices.
2. Stuff with onion, celery, garlic and thyme.
3. Place inside inner pot and add chicken broth.
4. Lock lid in place, select High Pressure and 30 minutes cooking time. When time is up use natural pressure release for 10 minutes, then do a quick pressure release to release any remaining pressure. Carefully remove the turkey breasts and plate them.
5. Strain and skim the fat off the broth if desired.
6. Whisk together corn starch and cold water then add to broth in inner pot.
7. Select Sauté and stir until broth thickens. Add salt and pepper to taste. Serve immediately.

Quick and Easy Korean Beef

Serving: 6

Total time taken: 55 min

Ingredients:

- 4 pounds bottom roast, cut into cubes
- Salt and pepper
- 2 tablespoons olive oil
- 1 cup beef broth
- ½ cup soy sauce
- 5 cloves garlic, minced
- 1 tablespoon fresh grated ginger
- 1 pear or Granny Smith apple peeled and chopped
- Juice or one large orange or 2 small

Directions:

1. Season the cubed roast liberally with salt and pepper.
2. Select Sauté. Once the pan is hot coat the pan with the olive oil and in batches brown the meat on all the sides. Transfer meat to a plate while you're working. Once all the meat is browned de-glaze the pan with the beef broth, scraping up all the browned bits.
3. Pour in the soy sauce and stir to combine.
4. Return all the meat back to the pan and then place the garlic, ginger and pear on top of the meat, stirring lightly to slightly combine.
5. Finally add in the orange juice. Place the lid on your Pressure Cooker and using the manual button on high pressure set to 45 minutes. Make sure the valve is closed. Once the pot is done, release the steam and shred meat using a fork.

Thai Green curry

Serving: 4

Total time taken: 1 hour

Ingredients:

- 3 pounds boneless skinless chicken thighs, cut into ½ inch pieces
- 1 tablespoon sesame oil
- 1 medium onion, peeled, and sliced thin
- 3 cloves garlic, crushed
- ½ inch piece of ginger, peeled and crushed
- 1 can (13.5 ounce) coconut milk
- 4 tablespoons green curry paste
- 1 teaspoon fine sea salt
- 1 cup chicken stock or water
- 1 tablespoon fish sauce
- 1 tablespoon soy sauce
- 1 tablespoon brown sugar
- Juice from 1 lime
- 12 ounces green beans, trimmed and cut into in halves

Directions:

1. Select Sauté and stir in the onion, garlic, and ginger, and sauté until the onion starts to soften, about 3 minutes.
2. Scoop the cream from the top of the can of coconut milk and add it to the pot, then stir in the curry paste. Cook, stirring often, until the curry paste darkens, about 5 minutes.
3. Sprinkle the chicken with the kosher salt. Add the chicken to the pot, and stir to coat with curry paste. Stir in the rest of the can of coconut milk, chicken stock, fish sauce, soy sauce, and brown sugar. Lock the lid and cook on High pressure for 10 minutes. When time is up do quick release the pressure in the pot.
4. Remove the lid then set Sauté mode. Stir in the lime juice and the green beans, and simmer the curry until the green beans are crisp-tender, about 4 minutes. Taste the curry as needed.

Ladle the curry into bowls, sprinkle with minced cilantro and basil, and serve with Jasmine rice.

Add Your Own Tips & Tricks

The Ultimate Beef Taco Bowl

Serving: 4

Total time taken: 15 min

Ingredients:

- 1 pound ground beef
- 2 cups white rice
- 1 ½ cups Hot Salsa
- 2 packets Hot Taco Seasons
- 2 cups canned black beans
- 2 cups shredded Monterey jack cheese
- 1 cup sour cream
- Sliced green onion for garnish
- Black Olives if desired
- 2 cups beef broth

Directions:

1. Select Sauté on Pressure Cooker add a drizzle of olive oil and brown the ground beef for 5 minutes.
2. Add 2 packets of taco seasons and beef broth. Add beans, and rice. Add salsa last on top.
3. Select Rice and default time to 12 minutes. Once time is up, do quick release and stir in the cheese until melted.
4. Serve into individual bowls. Garnish with sour cream, green onion, and black olives. Serve with nacho chips.

The All-American Meat Loaf

Serving: 4

Total time taken: 1 hour 10 min

Ingredients:

- 3 pounds lean ground beef
- 1 medium onion, roughly chopped
- 6 cloves garlic, roughly minced
- 2 extra large eggs, beaten
- 1½ teaspoon dried oregano
- 1½ teaspoon fennel seed, ground
- ¾ teaspoon Worcestershire sauce
- ¾ teaspoon kosher salt
- ¼ teaspoon black pepper
- ¾ cup panko bread crumbs
- 1 cup tomato sauce
- 1 cup chicken stock
- 1 cup tomato paste
- 1 potato, peeled and sliced into disks

Directions:

1. In large mixing bowl, mix together all the ingredients with your beef, except for the tomato sauce, tomato paste and chicken stock.
2. Form your meat mixture into a loaf. Set aside. Place your potato slices into inner pot by layering them. Then place your meat loaf on top of the potato slices. Add in the chicken stock. Lock lid and cook on High pressure for 40 minutes.
3. Once time is up, release pressure naturally then whisk in the tomato paste and tomato sauce and cook on High again for another 10 minutes. Use quick release.
4. Serve with rice and salad.

Mediterranean Beef Dinner

Serving: 4

Total time taken: 40 min

Ingredients:

- 2 pound beef roast
- 2 tablespoon olive oil
- 8 oz. jar pepperoncini
- 2 tablespoon minced garlic
- 2 cups beef broth
- Salt and pepper to taste

Directions:

1. Select Sauté, then season your roast with salt and pepper and rub it with minced garlic. Brown your roast on both sides in olive oil about 5 minutes each side.
2. Pour the broth over your roast and lock lid and select Meat/Stew button and default time to 35 minutes. Once time is up do quick release then add in the pepperoncini and lock lid and cook on High for 10 minutes. Do quick release and serve with pasta or rice.

Easy Easter Sunday Pot Roast

Serving: 4

Total time taken: 1 hour

Ingredients:

- 3 pound Beef Rump Roast
- 1 packet of Instant Gravy Powder
- 1 packet of Instant Ranch Dip Powder
- 2 tablespoon Worcestershire Sauce
- 1 shallot, chopped
- 2 cups beef broth
- 2 cups baby carrots
- 6 red potatoes, chopped
- 1 medium onion, sliced
- 1 cup white mushrooms, sliced

Directions:

1. In a large mixing bowl, season the roast with the gravy powder, ranch powder and Worcestershire sauce. Place roast inside inner pot then add in the beef broth and then lock lid and cook on High pressure for 45 minutes. Once time is up do quick release.
2. Add your vegetables into the inner pot and lock lid again and cook on High for another 15 minutes. Use natural release pressure.
3. Serve with rice or pasta or even warm dinner rolls.

Ragu Penne Pasta

Serving: 2

Total time taken: 20-30 min

Ingredients:

- 2 oz. Penne pasta
- 1 serving Four Cheese Sauce (One Jar)
- 1 cup beef stock
- ½ pound ground Sirloin
- 1 clove garlic, minced

Directions:

1. Select Sauté setting in Pressure Cooker, add a drizzle of olive oil and brown the ground Sirloin for about 5 minutes. Add in the Four Cheese Sauce and mix well. Then add in the pasta and the beef stock and minced garlic.
2. Lock lid and select Meat/Stew and adjust to 25 minutes.
3. Once time is up do quick release, give everything a stir and taste for seasoning. Serve with salad.

Spaghetti Squash and Meat Sauce

Serving: 2

Total time taken: 30 min

Ingredients:

- 1 pound ground beef
- 1 small chopped onion
- 3 cloves minced garlic
- 1 teaspoon kosher salt
- 28 oz. can crushed tomatoes
- 1 Bay leaf
- 1 Large spaghetti squash
- Grated cheddar cheese for topping

Directions:

1. Select Sauté and brown the beef with onion, garlic, salt, pepper. Added crushed tomatoes, bay leaf and cheese rind, stir.
2. Pierce the spaghetti squash all over with a knife and place over the meat sauce. Select Slow Cook and set for 3 hours. Once time is up do quick release and let the squash cool before removing.
3. Split squash with knife and remove flesh with large fork
4. Place the spaghetti squash on serving platter and top it off with the meat sauce.

Spanish Chorizo and Peppers

Serving: 6

Total time taken: 40-50 min

Ingredients:

- 3 pounds chorizo sausages
- 2 cups crushed tomatoes
- 1 cup tomato sauce
- 1 cup red wine
- ½ teaspoon smoked paprika
- ¼ teaspoon red pepper flakes
- 1 teaspoon sea salt
- ½ teaspoon fresh cracked pepper
- 1 teaspoon minced garlic
- 2 tablespoons extra virgin olive oil
- 1 large Sweet onion, sliced
- 3 large Red Bells Peppers, cored and sliced

Directions:

1. Add all ingredients to Pressure Cooker.
2. Stir well, then lock lid and select Meat/Stew and default time to 45 minutes.
3. Once time is up do quick release and serve with rice or dinner rolls.

Country Style Pork Chop Casserole

Serving: 4

Total time taken: 35 min

Ingredients:

- 4 1-inch pork chops
- Salt and pepper
- ¼ cup chicken stock
- 4 medium potatoes, peeled sliced into rounds
- 1 onion, thinly sliced
- ¾ cup white wine
- 1 finely crushed bay leaf
- 1 teaspoon garlic powder
- 1 teaspoon dried parsley flakes

Directions:

1. Season pork chops generously with salt and pepper and set aside.
2. Layer the potatoes into the bottom of the inner pot then lay your pork chops on top of the potatoes. Add in the chicken stock and white wine and the rest of the seasoning spice.
3. Lick lid and cook on High for 20 minutes. Once time is up let it release pressure naturally and serve with salad or pasta.

Pork Medallions and Mushrooms

Serving: 4

Total time taken: 20-30 min

Ingredients:

- 2 pork tenderloins; cleaned and sliced into 2 cm medallions
- 2 sprigs fresh rosemary
- 3 sprigs fresh thyme
- 3 cups cremini mushrooms; sliced
- 2 cups chicken stock
- Olive oil
- Flour, salt, and pepper for dredging

Directions:

1. Mix approximately ½ cup flour with 1 teaspoon salt and ½ teaspoon freshly ground black pepper.
2. Heat olive oil in the Pressure Cooker using the Sauté button. Dredge each pork medallion in the flour mixture and brown each side in the Pressure Cooker.
3. Remove the browned medallions and add the fresh herbs. Deglaze the inner pot with the chicken stock for a couple of minutes, scraping the bottom to loosen all the bits.
4. Return the medallions to the Pressure Cooker, add the mushrooms on top. Lock lid and cook on High for 15 minutes. Let it naturally release pressure. Serve with salad or rice on the side.

Herb Garlic Leg of Lamb

Serving: 4

Total time taken: 50 min

Ingredients:

- 2 pound Leg of Lamb, boneless
- Fresh rosemary and lavender
- 1 tablespoon mixed garlic and onion powder
- 1 onion, chopped
- 2 russet potatoes, peeled and chopped into large chunks
- 2 teaspoon sesame oil
- 2 cups chicken broth

Directions:

1. Rub lamb leg with the herbs, garlic and onion powder and sesame oil. Place into inner pot and add in the chicken broth. Select Meat/Stew and default time to 40 minutes. Once time is up let it naturally release pressure.
2. Add in the onions and potatoes and lock lid and cook on High for 10 minutes. Let it naturally release pressure.
3. Set lamb leg onto serving plate and serve with rice or salad.

Moroccan Lamb and Chickpeas

Serving: 4

Total time taken: 20-30 min

Ingredients:

- 1 pound lean ground lamb
- 2 teaspoons olive oil
- 2 cups baby carrots
- 1 medium onion, sliced
- ¾ teaspoon ground cumin
- ¾ teaspoon ground cinnamon
- ½ teaspoon ground coriander
- ¼ teaspoon ground red pepper
- 2 cups chicken broth
- 3 tablespoons tomato paste
- 1 ½ tablespoons lemon zest
- ¼ teaspoon salt
- 2 cups chickpeas, rinsed and drained
- ½ cup chopped fresh cilantro
- 1 tablespoon fresh lemon juice

Directions:

1. Season the lamb with cumin, cinnamon, coriander, red pepper and salt. Select Sauté add in the olive oil and quickly brown the ground lamb for 5 minutes.
2. Add in the rest of the ingredients, not including the cilantro and lemon juice. Lock lid and select Meat/Stew and adjust time to 25 minutes.
3. Once time is up, release pressure naturally then add in the lemon juice. Serve with fresh cilantro and over rice or pasta.

Pressure Cooker Seafood Recipes

Pressure Cooker Seafood Recipes

All about Seafood

SEAFOOD	ELECTRIC PRESSURE COOKER (10-12PSI)	STOVETOP PRESSURE COOKER (13-15PSI)	PRESSURE SELECTION	OPENING METHOD
Calamari	20	15 to 18	High	Normal
Carp	6	4	High	Normal
Clams, canned/jarred	add after pressure cooking			Normal
Clams, fresh	6	4	High	Normal
Cod	3	3	Low	Normal
Crab	3	2	Low	Normal
Eel	10	8	High	Normal
Fish fillet	3	2	Low	Normal
Fish soup or stock	6	5	High	Normal
Fish steak	4	3	High	Normal
Fish, mixed pieces (for fish soup)	8	6	Low	Normal
Fish, whole, gutted	6	5	Low	Normal
Fish, in packet (Al Cartoccio)	15	12	High	Normal
Frog's Legs	8	8	High	Normal
Haddock	7	6	Low	Normal
Halibut	7	6	Low	Normal
Lobster	12	8	Low	Normal
Lobster, 2 lb (1k)	3	2	Low	Normal
Mussels	1	1	Low	Normal
Ocean Perch	7	6	Low	Normal
Octopus	20	15	High	Normal, Natural
Oysters	6	4	Low	Normal
Perch	6	4	Low	Normal
Prawns (see Shrimp)				
Salmon	6	5	Low	Normal

Singapore Green Fish Curry

Serving: 4

Total time taken: 20 min

Ingredients:

- 2 pounds cod cut into thick strips
- 1 tablespoon sesame oil
- 3 shallots, thinly sliced
- 2 cloves garlic, crushed
- 3 tablespoon green curry paste
- 2 cups coconut milk
- 3 cups fish stock
- 2 tablespoon fish sauce
- 12 cherry tomatoes, halved
- Handful green beans, trimmed
- Fresh coriander, to serve
- 2 limes, quartered, to serve

Directions:

1. Add all the ingredients into the Pressure Cooker not including the lime and coriander leaves. Stir well.
2. Lock lid and cook on High for 25 minutes. Let it naturally release pressure.
3. Stir contents and taste for seasoning. Then stir in the fresh coriander leaves.
4. Divide into bowls and serve with side of lime and rice.

Lemon Pepper Tilapia with Asparagus

Serving: 4

Total time taken: 20-30 min

Ingredients:

- 1 bundle asparagus, ends cut
- 4 tilapia filets
- 8-12 tablespoons Lemon Juice
- 1 tablespoon lemon pepper seasoning
- ½ tablespoon butter for each filet

Directions:

1. Take 8 pieces of foil that will fit the size of your fish and asparagus. Lay out the first 4 packets. Place each fish on a foil then evenly distribute the asparagus and seasoning over your fish filets.
2. Place the second piece of foil over the filets and seal the sides tightly.
3. Place foil packets in cooking pot, they can overlap.
4. Lock lid and cook on High for 25 minutes. Once time is up, let it release pressure naturally.
5. Serve with rice or over pasta.

Spicy Lemon Salmon

Serving: 2

Total time taken: 10 min

Ingredients:

- 4 salmon filets
- 2 lemons, juice one and slice the other one
- 2 tablespoons Japanese Togarashi (assorted chili pepper)
- Sea Salt, to taste
- 1 cup water

Directions:

1. Pour 1 cup water into inner pot, place steamer basket into inner pot. Layer the fish in the basket and sprinkle your seasoning then lay the sliced lemon over each filet.
2. Lock lid and cook on High for 5 minutes. When time is up let it naturally release pressure.
3. Serve with a side of veggies and brown rice.

Greek Tuna Noodle Delight

Serving: 4

Total time taken: 20 min

Ingredients:

- 1 can of tuna fish in water, drained
- 1 cup drained diced tomatoes
- ½ cup of chopped red onion
- 1 cup marinated artichoke hearts, drained and chopped
- 8 ounces of dry wide egg noodles (uncooked)
- 1 cup fish stock
- Salt and pepper to taste
- Crumpled feta cheese
- Fresh chopped parsley for garnish

Directions:

1. Select Sauté and sauté the onions for about 5 minutes.
2. Add in the rest of your ingredients, except for the feta and parsley. Lock lid and select Soup and adjust time to 20 minutes. Once time is up do quick release.
3. Give everything a stir. Serve in bowls with the feta and fresh parsley.

Salmon and Scalloped Potatoes

Serving: 4-6

Total time taken: 15 min

Ingredients:

- 6 salmon filets
- 1 cup chicken broth
- 6 medium sized potatoes, peeled and cut into ¼ inch slices
- ½ teaspoon salt
- ⅛ teaspoon white pepper
- 1 tablespoon chopped chives
- ⅓ cup sour cream
- Dash of Paprika

Directions:

1. Season salmon with the salt and white pepper and paprika. Set aside.
2. Layer the potatoes into inner pot, then add in the chicken broth. Lay the filets on top of the potatoes and lock lid. Cook on High for 20 minutes.
3. Once time is up, naturally release pressure and serve with sprinkle of chopped chives and sour cream.

Lemon Ginger Mahi-Mahi

Serving: 2

Total time taken: 10 min

Ingredients:

- 2 mahi-mahi fillets
- Salt and pepper for seasoning
- 2 cloves garlic, minced
- 1 tablespoon ginger, finely grated
- 1 teaspoon lemon pepper seasoning
- ½ lime, juiced
- 2 tablespoons honey
- 1 tablespoon Japanese Togarashi
- 2 tablespoons sriracha
- 1 lemon, cut into slices

Directions:

1. Season the mahi-mahi with pinch of salt and pepper and the lemon pepper. In a separate bowl, whisk together minced garlic, ginger, lime juice, honey, sriracha and Togarashi. Set aside.
2. Lay your filets into inner pot then lay lemon slices on top of the fish and pour the whisked sauce over the fish.
3. Lick lid and cook on High for 15 minutes. Let it naturally release pressure.
4. Serve over a bed of rice or fresh greens.

Shrimp Fried Rice

Serving: 6

Total time taken: 20-30 min

Ingredients:

- 1 12 ounce bag frozen shrimp peeled and tailed
- 2 cups brown rice
- 2 large eggs
- 1 cup chopped onions
- 4 cloves garlic
- 1 and ½ cups frozen peas and carrots
- ½ teaspoon ground ginger
- ¼ cup soy sauce
- 2 cups fish stock
- Salt and pepper to taste

Directions:

1. Select Sauté button on the Pressure Cooker and let heat for a couple of minutes. Add a drizzle of olive oil. Once you hear the sesame oil bubbling, add the two beaten eggs and scramble them. Remove from pot and add another drizzle of olive oil. Add the chopped onion and minced garlic and sauté until translucent.
2. Then add shrimp and peas and carrots, then add the rice into the pot, Stir in the fish stock and soy. Lock lid and select Rice. Once timer goes off, stir in the scrambled eggs and serve.

Curry Coconut Cilantro Shrimp

Serving: 4-6

Total time taken: 20 min

Ingredients:

- 1 pound shrimp, with shells, rinsed
- 3 cups light coconut milk
- 1 cup water
- ½ cup Thai red curry sauce
- 2½ teaspoon lemon garlic seasoning
- ¼ cup packed fresh cilantro leaves

Directions:

1. Add all ingredients into inner pot. Stir well.
2. Lock lid and select Bean/Chili and default time to 30 minutes. Once time is up do quick release.
3. Then add in the cilantro leaves and stir. Serve over rice or noodles.

Seafood Coconut Curry

Serving: 4-6

Total time taken: 15-20 min

Ingredients:

- 2 tablespoons sesame oil
- 1 onion, thinly sliced
- 1 garlic clove, crushed
- 2cm piece ginger, grated
- 2 tablespoons mild curry paste
- 1 tablespoon tomato puree
- 10 prawns, peeled, tails intact
- 1 pound Manila clams, scrubbed and washed
- 2 cans coconut milk
- 1 cup chicken stock
- 2 tablespoons lime juice
- 2 tablespoons chopped coriander leaves

Directions:

1. In large mixing bowl combine the following and set aside:
- 2 tablespoons sesame oil
- 1 onion, thinly sliced
- 1 garlic clove, crushed
- 2cm piece ginger, grated
- 2 tablespoons mild curry paste

- 1 tablespoon tomato puree
- 10 prawns, peeled, tails intact
- 1 pound Manila clams, scrubbed and washed

2. Set pressure cooker on High and add the chicken stock and coconut milk and the seafood mixture. Cook on High for 15 minutes. Set timer.
3. Once timer goes off release pressure naturally. Give it a good stir and adjust seasoning to taste, and serve with coriander leaves and lime juice.

Scoville Units	Pepper
15,000,000 – 16,000,000	Pure Capsaicin
5,000,000 – 5,300,000	Pepper Spray
855,000 – 1,500,000	Ghost Pepper (Bhut Jolokia, Naga Jolokia)
350,000 – 580,000	Red Savina Habanero Pepper
100,000 – 350,000	Habanero, Scotch Bonnet Peppers
30,000 – 50,000	Cayenne, Tabasco Peppers
3,500 – 8,000	Jalapeño Pepper
100 – 900	Pimento, Banana Peppers
0	Bell Pepper

Milk Fish Curry

Serving: 6

Total time taken: 15 min

Ingredients:

- 1 ½ pounds haddock (or another mild white fish), cut into pieces
- 2 tablespoons coconut oil, divided
- ½ teaspoon mustard seeds
- 1 onion, diced
- 1 serrano, chopped
- 5 garlic cloves, chopped
- 1 inch ginger, chopped
- ½ cup water
- 1 teaspoon coriander powder
- ½ teaspoon paprika
- ½ teaspoon turmeric
- ½ teaspoon garam masala
- 1 teaspoon salt
- ½ teaspoon tamarind paste
- ½ cup coconut milk
- Chopped cilantro, for garnish

Directions:

1. Melt 1 tablespoon of coconut oil in pressure cooker and sauté the mustard seeds. Once the mustard seeds begin to pop, add the onion and serrano pepper. Cook for 8-10 minutes, until the onions begin to brown. Then add the garlic and ginger, stir then turn off heat.

2. Scoop everything from out of the pressure cooker and put it into a food processor or blender along with the water. Puree until smooth. Pour this back into pressure cooker add the spices and the fish along with the tamarind paste and coconut milk. Lock lid and cook on High for 15 minutes. Set timer.
3. Once timer goes off, release pressure naturally, give the curry a stir making sure the fish is cooked through. Serve over rice and garnish with cilantro and serve.

Scoville Units	Pepper
15,000,000 – 16,000,000	Pure Capsaicin
5,000,000 – 5,300,000	Pepper Spray
855,000 – 1,500,000	Ghost Pepper (Bhut Jolokia, Naga Jolokia)
350,000 – 580,000	Red Savina Habanero Pepper
100,000 – 350,000	Habanero, Scotch Bonnet Peppers
30,000 – 50,000	Cayenne, Tabasco Peppers
3,500 – 8,000	Jalapeño Pepper
100 – 900	Pimento, Banana Peppers
0	Bell Pepper

Seafood and Fish	Fresh, Cooking Time (in Minutes)	Frozen, Cooking Time (in Minutes)
Crab	3 – 4	5 – 6
Fish, whole (trout, snapper, etc.)	5 – 6	7 – 10
Fish fillet,	2 – 3	3 – 4
Fish steak	3 – 4	4 – 6
Lobster	3 – 4	4 – 6
Mussels	2 – 3	4 – 5
Seafood soup or stock	6 – 7	7 – 9
Shrimp or Prawn	1 – 2	2 – 3

Clam Linguine

Serving: 2

Total time taken: 15

Ingredients:

- 2 pounds Manila clams, scrubbed (try to get them all the same size)
- 2 inches dried linguini, broken in half
- 2 cups halved cherry tomatoes
- 2 tablespoons olive oil
- 1 medium red onion, thinly sliced
- 2 tablespoons sea salt
- 1 tablespoon sesame oil
- 1 cup sake or white wine
- 1 pinch of dried red chili flakes
- 3 cloves garlic, minced
- 4 cups fish stock
- ½ cup chopped fresh parsley leaves
- 1 tablespoon fresh lemon zest
- Fresh lemon wedges to serve

Directions:

1. Heat the oil in pressure cooker and sauté the onion with the salt until tender, then add in the garlic and sauté for another 1 minute.
2. Add in the fish stock, linguine, cherry tomatoes, sake, and sesame oil. Spread out the clams over the linguine. Lock lid and cook on High for 10 minutes. Set timer. Once timer goes off,

release pressure naturally and check the pasta for tenderness and that the clams are fully open, it not cook on High for another 2-5 minutes.

3. Serve in shallow plates with fresh parsley, lemon zest and lemon wedges.

Cod Chowder

Serving: 6

Total time taken: 25 min

Ingredients:

- 2 tablespoon butter
- 1 cup Onion, chopped
- ½ Mushrooms, sliced
- 4 cups Potatoes, peeled & diced
- 4 cups chicken broth
- 2 pounds frozen cod
- 1 tablespoon Old Bay Seasoning (or more)
- Salt & Pepper to taste
- 1 cup clam juice
- ½ cup flour
- 1 cup Half & Half or, 1 can Evaporated Milk

Directions:

1. Add all the liquids into pressure cooker first then lay out your frozen cod.
2. Place the potatoes and mushrooms over the cod and add your seasoning. Lock lid and cook on High for 20 minutes. Set timer. Once timer goes off release pressure naturally, and give your chowder a gentle stir breaking up the cod into bite size bits with your wooden spoon.
3. Season to taste and lock lid and cook on High for another 5 minutes. Set timer. Once timer goes off release pressure and serve hot with your favorite dinner rolls.

Prawn Risotto

Serving: 2-4

Total time taken: 30 min

Ingredients:

- ½ pound frozen tiger prawns, thawed and peeled
- 1 teaspoon salt
- 1 teaspoon white pepper
- 3 tablespoons olive oil
- 4 tablespoons butter
- 1 shallot, minced
- 3 cloves garlic, minced
- 2 cups Arborio rice
- ¾ cup cooking sake
- 2 teaspoons soy sauce
- 4 cups fish stock or Japanese Dashi
- 20 grams Parmesan cheese, finely grated
- 2 finely chopped green onion stalks

Directions:

1. In mixing bowl season the prawns with salt and white pepper. Set pressure cooker on High and add the olive oil and butter and sauté prawns for 5-10 minutes with the shallot and garlic, the prawns should be about 80% cooked. Remove and set aside.
2. Add the Arborio rice, cooking sake, soy sauce and fish stock into pressure cooker with a swirl of olive oil. Stir and combine, make sure the rice is coated with the liquids. Or Japanese Dashi
3. Once timer goes off release pressure naturally and place the prawns on top of the risotto and sprinkle the parmesan cheese over the prawns and risotto. Cover and lock lid again and cook on High for another 5 minutes. Set timer.
4. Once timer goes off release pressure naturally and serve. Garnish with the sliced green onions

Pressure Cooker Crab Legs

Serving: 2

Total time taken: 30 min

Ingredients:

- 3 bunches crab leg (snow, per person)
- 1/2 cups butter (melted)
- 4 cloves garlic (minced)
- 1 teaspoon dill
- Lemon slices
- Butter

Directions:

1. Rinse Snow crab legs or King crab legs under running water, place legs in pot fitted with a pan or dish and put water crockpot in until it comes 1/2 way up to the pan and legs can steam. (You want to steam them) If desired saw or cut King crab legs in appetizer size pieces before or after cooking, your choice.
2. Melt the 1/2 cup butter in a small bowl and mix in the garlic and dill. Pour mixture over crab legs in pan. Cover; cook on low for 1- 2 hours.
3. Serve with lemon and melted butter with a little garlic powder added.

Pressure Cooker

Vegetarian Recipes

Vegetable	Fresh, Cooking Time (in Minutes)	Frozen, Cooking Time (in Minutes)
Artichoke, whole, trimmed without leaves	9 – 11	11 – 13
Artichoke, hearts	4 – 5	5 – 6
Asparagus, whole or cut	1 – 2	2 – 3
Beans, green/yellow or wax, whole, trim ends and strings	1 – 2	2 – 3
Beets, small roots, whole	11 – 13	13 – 15
Beets, large roots, whole	20 – 25	25 – 30
Broccoli, flowerets	2 – 3	3 – 4
Broccoli, stalks	3 – 4	4 – 5
Brussel sprouts, whole	3 – 4	4 – 5
Cabbage, red, purple or green, shredded	2 – 3	3 – 4
Cabbage, red, purple or green, wedges	3 – 4	4 – 5
Carrots, sliced or shredded	1 – 2	2 – 3
Carrots, whole or chunked	2 – 3	3 – 4
Cauliflower flowerets	2 – 3	3 – 4
Celery, chunks	2 – 3	3 – 4
Collard	4 – 5	5 – 6
Corn, kernels	1 – 2	2 – 3
Corn, on the cob	3 – 4	4 – 5
Eggplant, slices or chunks	2 – 3	3 – 4

PRESSURE COOKER COOKING

Pressure Cooker Enchilada Quinoa

Servings: 4

Total time taken: 2 hrs.

Ingredients:

- 2 cups black beans, drained, rinsed
- 3 cups mild or medium red enchilada sauce
- 2 cups corn tidbits
- 1 cup diced fire roasted tomatoes with green chilies
- ½ cup quinoa, uncooked
- ¼ cup vegetable broth
- 1 cup shredded cheddar cheese
- 2 tablespoons fresh cilantro, chopped
- 2 tablespoons sour cream
- 2 tomatoes, chopped
- 1 avocado, peeled, pitted, sliced

Directions:

1. Add all the beans, corn quinoa and fire roasted tomatoes and green chilies and add in the vegetable broth and enchilada sauce. Lock lid and select Meat/Stew default time to 1 hour.
2. When time is up do quick release, spoon everything into a large bowl. Sprinkle cheddar cheese, chopped tomatoes and lay the slices of avocado on top and then add the sour cream on top of everything.
3. Serve immediately with warm tortilla chips for dipping.

Rustic Vegetable Gratin

Servings: 2

Total time taken: 1 hr.

Ingredients:

- 1 golden squash or yellow squash, chopped
- 1 red bell pepper, cored and sliced
- 1 green bell pepper, cored and sliced
- 1 onion, chopped
- 1½ tablespoons olive oil
- 1 clove garlic, minced
- 6 tomatoes, sliced
- 2 tablespoons fresh basil leaves, finely chopped
- ½ cup parmesan cheese
- Salt and pepper

Directions:

1. Switch on the Pressure Cooker.
2. Add all the ingredients except the tomatoes into the inner pot. Mix well.
3. Close the lid. Select the Slow Cook function and set the timer for 1 hour. Once time is up do quick release. Spoon everything into a dish and lay the tomatoes slices on top of the gratin. Serve with warm dinner rolls.

Swiss chard with Chickpeas and Couscous

Servings: 6

Total time taken: 1 hour

Ingredients:

- 4 cups couscous
- 3 cups boiling water
- 4 bunches Swiss chard, trimmed
- 4 cups canned chickpeas, rinsed, drained
- 1 cup raisins
- 1 cup pine nuts, toasted
- 4 cloves garlic, sliced
- 1/3 cup olive oil
- Salt to taste
- Pepper powder to taste

Directions:

1. Transfer the couscous into a large bowl. Pour hot water and mix well. Fluff with a fork. Cover, set aside. Select Sauté option. Add oil and garlic and sauté until fragrant.
2. Add the rest of the ingredients except pine nuts. Close the lid. Press Multi-grain function and default time to 40 minutes.
3. Divide the couscous into individual plates. Place the cooked chard and garnish with pine nuts and serve.

Mix Vegetable Curry with Tofu

Servings: 4

Total time taken: 20 min

Ingredients:

- 2 small egg plants, chopped
- 1 large onion, chopped
- 24 ounces extra firm tofu, drained, pressed of excess moisture, cut into small squares
- ½ cup frozen peas
- 1 green bell pepper, sliced
- 1 red bell pepper, sliced
- 2 teaspoons fresh ginger, minced
- 3 tablespoon red curry paste
- 1 cup coconut milk
- 1 cup vegetable broth
- ¼ teaspoon turmeric powder
- Salt to taste

Directions:

1. Add all the ingredients to the cooking pot and mix well.
2. Close the lid. Select the Steam default time to 15 minutes.
3. Let the steam release naturally for 8 minutes.
4. When done, serve over hot cooked brown rice.

Vegetable Succotash

Servings: 6-8

Total time taken: 15 min

Ingredients:

- 3 cups zucchini, diced
- 3 cups corn kernels
- 1 cup onion, diced
- 2 cups okra, sliced
- 6 cloves garlic, minced
- 4 tablespoons lemon juice
- 4 cups of canned, seasoned diced tomatoes in juice
- Salt and pepper to taste
- 1 cup vegetable broth
- 1 teaspoon hot sauce
- ½ teaspoon red pepper flakes
- 2 tablespoons fresh parsley, chopped

Directions:

1. Add tomatoes with juice and broth to the inner pot.
2. Add corn, okra, zucchini, onions, garlic, salt, pepper and red pepper flakes and mix well.
3. Close the lid. Press Steam function and use the default time of 10 minutes. Quick release the pressure when complete.
4. Add parsley, lemon juice and hot sauce and mix well.
5. Serve hot as it is or over rice.

Mixed Vegetable Curry

Servings: 2

Total time taken: 20 min

Ingredients:

- 2 carrots, medium sized, sliced
- 1 potato, cut into ½ inch cubes
- 2 cups corn tidbits
- ½ pound fresh string beans, cut into 1 inch pieces
- ½ cup onion, coarsely chopped
- 2 cloves garlic, minced
- 2 teaspoons curry powder
- ¼ teaspoon red chili flakes
- ½ teaspoon coriander, powdered
- 1 big pinch cinnamon powder
- 1 cup vegetable broth
- 1 cup thick coconut milk

Directions:

1. Add the vegetables, and seasoning and liquids into inner pot.
2. Lock lid and press Steam function and use the default time of 10 minutes. Let the steam release naturally. Stir well, and serve over hot rice or with crusty warm bread.

Peas Risotto

Servings: 2

Total time taken: 30 min

Ingredients:

- 1 cup Arborio rice
- 1 medium onion, chopped
- 1 cup frozen peas
- 2 cups vegetable broth
- 4 tablespoons parmesan cheese
- 2 tablespoons butter
- Salt and to taste
- Pepper to taste

Directions:

1. Using Sauté mode, add butter to inner pot then add onions and sauté until translucent.
2. Add broth and peas then stir well. Lock lid. Select the Rice function. When cycle is complete, add, salt, pepper, extra butter and cheese. Mix well and serve with side of salad.

Asian Crunchy Noodle Salad Bowl

Servings: 6

Total time taken: 20 min

Ingredients:

- 1 ½ pounds thin spaghetti
- 1 ½ cups bean sprouts
- 4 scallions, sliced
- 1 red bell pepper, thinly sliced
- 1 green bell pepper, thinly sliced

Sauce:

- 1/3 cup rice wine vinegar
- 1/3 cup sesame oil
- ½ cup soy sauce
- 1½ tablespoons honey
- 1¼ cups crunchy peanut butter
- 5 tablespoons sesame oil
- 3 teaspoons fresh ginger, grated
- 3 cloves garlic, grated
- 5 tablespoons roasted peanuts to garnish
- Cilantro leaves to garnish

Directions:

1. Add spaghetti and 6 cups of water into the inner pot.
2. Lock lid and press Steam and adjust the timer down to 3 minutes. Quick release the pressure.
3. Rinse and place in a bowl.
4. Add the rest of the ingredients into inner pot and ¼ cup water. Select Steam function and adjust the timer down to 3 minutes again.
5. Perform a quick release, then add to the noodles.
6. Whisk together the sauce ingredients in a bowl and pour over the noodles. Toss well, garnish with peanuts and cilantro and serve.

Quick Spinach & Corn Au Gratin

Servings: 4

Total time taken: 20-35 min

Ingredients:

- 1½ cups frozen corn
- 1 pound baby spinach leaves
- 2 teaspoons garlic, minced
- ¼ cup flour
- 3 cups cold milk
- 2 tablespoons butter
- ½ cup cheese, grated or more if you like it cheesy
- 1 tablespoon of mixed season: salt, red chili flakes, oregano, and pepper to taste

Directions:

1. On Sauté function. Add butter. When it melts, add garlic and sauté until fragrant and then add flour and sauté for 30 seconds.
2. Add cold milk while whisking simultaneously.
3. Press the Adjust button twice. Simmer until thick. Add salt and pepper and whisk again until it is free of lumps. Then add rest of ingredients and stir for 5 minutes.
4. Lock lid and cook on High pressure for 25 minutes. Once time is up release pressure naturally and serve over warm crusty bread.

Pressure Cooker Vegetable Lasagna

Servings: 4

Total time taken: 30 min

Ingredients:

- 1 jar (24 ounce) Italian tomato sauce
- 5-6 thick lasagna noodles, broken
- 1 large green bell pepper, chopped
- 1 large red bell pepper, chopped
- 2 large carrots, chopped
- 1 cup frozen corn, thawed
- 1 medium zucchini, thinly sliced
- 12 ounce part skim ricotta cheese
- 1 cup Mozzarella cheese, shredded
- ½ cup parmesan cheese, shredded
- 2 tablespoons fresh parsley
- Salt to taste

Directions:

1. Spray the inner pot with cooking spray. Spread about ½ cup of tomato sauce at the bottom of the pot.
2. Lay about 1/3 of the lasagna pieces over it.
3. Make layers by spreading about 1/3 of each of the following; vegetables, salt, sauce, ricotta cheese, mozzarella cheese and lasagna. Repeat the above step twice.

4. Finally spread a thin layer of sauce and top with Parmesan cheese. Close the lid. Select the Multi-grain function and adjust to 20 minutes. Let it natural release. Sprinkle parsley over it. Slice and serve.

Vegetable	Fresh, Cooking Time (in Minutes)	Frozen, Cooking Time (in Minutes)
Artichoke, whole, trimmed without leaves	9 – 11	11 – 13
Artichoke, hearts	4 – 5	5 – 6
Asparagus, whole or cut	1 – 2	2 – 3
Beans, green/yellow or wax, whole, trim ends and strings	1 – 2	2 – 3
Beets, small roots, whole	11 – 13	13 – 15
Beets, large roots, whole	20 – 25	25 – 30
Broccoli, flowerets	2 – 3	3 – 4
Broccoli, stalks	3 – 4	4 – 5
Brussel sprouts, whole	3 – 4	4 – 5
Cabbage, red, purple or green, shredded	2 – 3	3 – 4
Cabbage, red, purple or green, wedges	3 – 4	4 – 5
Carrots, sliced or shredded	1 – 2	2 – 3
Carrots, whole or chunked	2 – 3	3 – 4
Cauliflower flowerets	2 – 3	3 – 4
Celery, chunks	2 – 3	3 – 4
Collard	4 – 5	5 – 6
Corn, kernels	1 – 2	2 – 3

Home-style Broccoli and Rice Casserole

Servings: 2

Total time taken: 1 hour

Ingredients:

- ½ pound broccoli florets, finely chopped
- ¾ cup brown rice, uncooked
- 1 ¼ cup water
- 1 cup mushrooms, finely chopped
- 1 tablespoon butter
- 2 tablespoons onions, finely chopped
- 1 clove garlic, minced
- 1 cup milk
- 1 tablespoon flour
- ½ cup low fat cheddar cheese, divided
- 2 tablespoons parmesan cheese, grated

Directions:

1. Add all the ingredients into thinner pot. Give everything quick stir.
2. Lock lid and choose Multi-grain and use the default time of 40 minutes. Once time is up do quick release. Serve with extra parmesan.

Easy Veggie Enchilada Orzo

Servings: 6

Total time taken: 30 min

Ingredients:

- 2 cups fire roasted diced tomatoes
- 2 cups chopped green chilies, drained
- 2 cups enchilada sauce
- 1½ cups canned black beans
- 1½ cups corn
- 2 cups vegetable broth
- 3 cups orzo pasta
- 6 ounces cream cheese, cubed
- 4 tablespoons fresh cilantro, chopped

Directions:

1. Add tomatoes, enchilada sauce, green chilies, broth, corn, salt, pepper and black beans to pot and stir. Place the cream cheese cubes all over.
2. Lock lid and cook on High for 15 minutes. When time is up do quick release. Then stir in the orzo lock lid and cook on High again for another 15 minutes. Do quick release, stir and adjust for seasoning.
3. Sprinkle cilantro and serve.

Asian Tofu Salad

Servings: 4

Total time taken: 40 min

Ingredients:

- 2 cups chickpeas, rinsed
- 1 cup cooked elbow pasta
- 1 cup frozen corn, thawed
- 1 large tomato, chopped
- 1 apple, chopped
- 1 cup tofu, chopped
- 1 green bell pepper, chopped

For the dressing:

- 3 tablespoons apple cider vinegar
- Pepper powder to taste
- ½ teaspoon red chili flakes
- 1 clove garlic, minced
- 1 teaspoon dried oregano
- Sesame seed for garnish

Directions:

1. Add the chickpeas and salt to the inner pot. Add enough water to cover the chickpeas, lock lid press Bean/Chili function and set time to 25 minutes. Let the steam release naturally.
2. Drain and transfer into a large bowl and cool.
3. Meanwhile, whisk together all the ingredients for dressing in a bowl and set aside.

4. Add the rest of the ingredients into the bowl with the chickpeas. Pour dressing on top and toss well and serve.

Add Your Own Tips & Tricks

Vegetarian Shepherd's Pie

Servings: 6-8

Total time taken: 1 hr. 40 min

Ingredients:

For mashed potatoes layer:
- 1 ½ pounds Yukon gold potatoes, thoroughly washed, halved
- 2 tablespoons butter
- Salt to taste
- Pepper powder to taste

For the lentil layer:
- ¾ cup green lentils, rinsed
- 2 cups vegetable stock
- 1 onion, chopped
- 1 clove garlic, minced
- 5 ounce bag mixed frozen vegetables
- ½ teaspoon dried thyme
- ½ tablespoon olive oil

Directions:

1. Add potatoes to the inner pot. Add salt and cover with water. Select the Congee/Porridge change time to 15 minutes. Let the pressure release naturally then drain well and transfer into a bowl.
2. Mash with a potato masher until smooth. Add butter, salt and pepper. Partially cover and keep aside.
3. On Sauté. Add oil, onions and garlic and sauté until light golden brown. Add green lentils, vegetable stock, frozen vegetables, and thyme. Press the Cancel button.
4. Lock lid and cook on High for 15 minutes. Do quick release. Layer with the mashed potato layer.
5. Cover the lid and select the Slow Cook function and set the timer for 1 hour. Once time is up do quick release and serve with a side salad.

Spinach Tortillas

Servings: 4

Total time taken: 2 hrs.

Ingredients:

- 5 ounce frozen spinach, chopped, thawed, squeeze the excess liquid
- ½ cup corn tidbits
- ½ teaspoon cumin powder
- 1 cup shredded sharp cheddar cheese
- 1½ cup salsa
- 4 tortillas (8 inch), warmed
- 3 cups romaine lettuce, chopped
- 2 radishes, cut into matchsticks
- ¼ cup grape tomatoes, halved
- 1 ½ tablespoon fresh lemon juice
- 1 scallion, sliced

Directions:

1. In a large mixing bowl mash together the spinach, corn, lettuce, radish, tomatoes, lemon juice and cumin powder.
2. Divide this mixture among the 4 tortillas and roll it up.
3. Spread half the salsa at the bottom of the inner pot. With the seam side down, place it in the pot in a single layer. Pour the remaining salsa over it. Sprinkle the cheddar over it.
4. Lock lid and press Multi-grain function and use the default time of 40 minutes.
5. Let the pressure release naturally for 15 minutes. Serve with hot tortillas topped with scallions.

Creamy Mushroom Polenta

Servings: 6

Total time taken: 25 min

Ingredients:

- 2 cups polenta
- 2 tablespoons olive oil
- 1½ pounds mushrooms, sliced
- 1 onion, chopped
- Salt and pepper to taste
- 8 cups vegetable stock
- 4 tablespoons butter
- 2/3 cup cheese, grated

Directions:

1. Switch on the Pressure Cooker.
2. Add all the ingredients into the inner pot.
3. Close the lid. Select the Multi-grain function and down to 20 minutes.
4. Perform a quick release then stir and serve.

Vegetarian Tacos

Servings: 6-8

Total time taken: 35 min

Ingredients:

- 1 cup Portobello mushrooms, sliced
- 2 stalks celery, finely chopped
- 1 green chili, chopped
- 1 medium onion, finely chopped
- 1 medium green bell pepper, chopped
- 1 clove garlic, minced
- ¼ cup tomato puree
- ½ cup vegetable stock
- ½ tablespoon sesame oil
- 2 teaspoons taco seasoning
- 2 cups kidney beans, rinsed, drained
- 6-8 ready-made taco shells
- 1 cup sour cream
- 1 tablespoon cilantro, chopped
- ½ cup cheddar cheese, shredded

Directions:

1. Add all the ingredients except tacos shells into inner pot and stir well.
2. Select the Bean/Chili and use the default time of 30 minutes. Once time is up do quick release.
3. To fill the tacos: Spoon in about 2-3 tablespoons of the filling into each of the taco shells. Sprinkle cheese and cilantro. Top with sour cream and serve.

PRESSURE COOKER COOKING

Pressure Cooker Dessert Recipes

Peanut Butter Chocolate Cheesecake

Servings: 4

Total time taken: 25 min + chilling time

Ingredients:

- 3 eggs
- 24 ounces cream cheese, softened
- 2 tablespoons cocoa
- 3 tablespoons powdered peanut butter
- ¾ cup swerve sugar substitute
- 1 ½ teaspoons vanilla extract
- Whipped cream and peanut butter to top

Directions:

1. Add all the ingredients into a blender and blend until smooth. Divide and transfer into 4 mason jars. Cover with lid or foil. Pour 2 cups of water into the pot. Place a trivet in the pot.
2. Place the jars on the trivet inside the pot. Cook in batches if required.
3. Close the lid. Select Steam to 15 minutes. Let the steam release naturally then chill for a couple of hours and serve.

Mini Salted Caramel Mocha Cheesecakes

Servings: 8

Total time taken: 2 hrs. + Chilling time

Ingredients:

For mocha cheesecakes:

- 1 ½ cups ground chocolate graham crackers or chocolate wafers
- 2 large eggs
- ½ cup butter, melted
- 16 ounces cream cheese, softened
- 2/3 cup sugar
- 1 teaspoon instant coffee
- 2 ounces bittersweet chocolate, melted, slightly cooled
- ¼ teaspoon salt
- 1 teaspoon vanilla extract

- **For salted caramel:**
- 2 cups packed brown sugar
- 2 tablespoons vanilla extract
- 8 tablespoons unsalted butter
- 1 cup heavy whipping cream

Directions:

1. Spray 8 canning jars of 4 ounces each with cooking spray. Mix together in a bowl, crackers and butter. Press into jars. Add sugar and cream cheese to a large bowl and beat until smooth. Add eggs, chocolate, vanilla, coffee and salt and beat again. Pour into the jars (up to ¾).

2. Place the jars in the Pressure Cooker. Pour warm waterfall around the jars. The jars should be covered up to ¾ with water. Cook in batches if needed. Close the lid. Select the Slow cook function and set the timer for 1-½ hours. Perform a quick release then chill for a couple of hours.
3. Meanwhile, make the salted caramel as follows: Place a heavy bottomed saucepan over medium heat. Add butter, brown sugar, cream and salt. Stir constantly and cook until well blended. Add vanilla and simmer for a minute. Remove from heat and cool.
4. Spoon salted caramel over the cheesecake. Top with whipped cream and serve.

Add Your Own Tips & Tricks

Chocolate Fudge

Servings: 6

Total time taken: 1 hr. + chilling

Ingredients:

- 1 ¼ cups dark chocolate chips
- ¼ cup coconut milk
- 2 tablespoons honey
- 1 tablespoon coconut oil
- ½ teaspoon vanilla extract
- 2 tablespoons walnuts, chopped into small pieces

Directions:

1. Add all the ingredients to the inner pot. Mix well.
2. Close the lid. Select the Slow Cook function and set the timer for 1 hour.
3. Let it cool to room temperature. Now stir constantly for a few minutes. Transfer the mixture into a greased tin. Cover and refrigerate until the fudge is set. Chop and serve.

Cherry Dump Cake

Servings: 6

Total time taken: 1 hour

Ingredients:

- ½ yellow cake mix
- ¼ cup butter, melted
- 1 can (21 ounces) cherry pie filling

Directions:

1. Mix together cake mix and butter in a bowl. Pour the cherries into a greased inner pot. Pour batter over it.
2. Close the lid. Select the Multi-grain function and use the default time of 40 minutes.
3. Let the pressure release naturally for 15 minutes. Uncover, cool for a while. Slice and serve. Tastes great with vanilla ice-cream.

Mango Coconut Rice Pudding

Servings: 8-10

Total time taken: 15 min

Ingredients:

- 2 cups Arborio rice
- 2 cans light coconut milk
- 2/3 cup brown sugar
- 3 cups water
- 1 cup half and half
- ¼ teaspoon salt
- 2 ripe mangoes, peeled, cubed
- 2 teaspoons vanilla
- ½ cup almonds, chopped + extra to garnish
- ½ cup shredded coconut

Directions:

1. Add rice, water, coconut milk, brown sugar and salt to the cooking pot. Stir.
2. Close the lid. Cook on High and set the timer for 8 minutes.
3. Perform a quick release then add rest of the ingredients and stir. Chill if desired
4. Spoon into bowls. Garnish with almonds and serve.

Strawberry Pudding

Servings: 8

Total time taken: 1 hr. 20 min

Ingredients:

- 2 cups plain flour
- 2 eggs, beaten
- 3 teaspoons baking powder
- 1 pound strawberries, chopped into small pieces
- 5 tablespoons dried breadcrumbs
- 1 cup butter, chopped
- 1 cup granulated sugar
- 10 ounces milk

Directions:

1. Mix together the dry ingredients in a bowl. Add butter and mix. Add milk and eggs and beat well. Add strawberries and stir. Transfer into a greased baking tin. Place a trivet inside the inner pot. Pour 2 cups of water. Place the dish over the trivet.
2. Close the lid. Select the Multi-grain function and "Adjust" the timer up to 60 minutes.
3. Quick release the pressure then serve and enjoy. Chill if desired.

Chocolate Peppermint Pudding

Servings: 6-8

Total time taken: 45 min

Ingredients:

For cake:

- 1 ½ cups all-purpose flour
- 6 tablespoons cocoa
- 9 ounces melted dark chocolate
- 1 ½ tablespoons baking powder
- 3 eggs
- ½ teaspoon salt
- 1 ¼ cups brown sugar
- ¾ cup heavy cream
- ¾ cup butter at room temperature
- 1 ½ teaspoons vanilla
- 1 ½ teaspoons peppermint candy, finely ground +extra for topping

- **For glaze:**
- 1 ½ cup chocolate chips, semi-sweet
- ¾ cup heavy cream

Directions:

1. Beat butter and sugar in a bowl until sugar dissolves. Add an egg at a time and a little flour at a time and mix until well combined. Add rest of the ingredients and mix into a smooth batter.

2. Grease a pan and pour the batter into it. Cover with foil. Pour 2 cups of water in the inner pot and place at rivet in it. Place the pan over it. Close the lid. Select Multi-grain and change timer down to 20 minutes. When done, perform a quick release then remove the pan from the pot. Discard water.
3. For glaze: Add cream to the Pressure Cooker. Select the "Sauté" function and bring to a boil. Switch off the pot and add chocolate chips. Stir until it melts.
4. When the pudding is completely cooled, invert onto a plate. Pour glaze over the pudding. Sprinkle peppermint candy powder over it. Slice and serve.

Add Your Own Tips & Tricks

Mixed Berry Pudding

Servings: 6

Total time taken: 1 hr. 15 minutes min

Ingredients:

- ¼ pound red currants, halved
- ¼ pound raspberries
- ¼ pound strawberries, chopped
- ¼ pound plums, pitted, chopped
- 1 ½ cups water
- ¼ cup corn starch
- ½ cup red wine

Directions:

1. Set aside a cup of berries, and add the rest to thinner pot. Add sugar and stir.
2. Cover the lid. Press Slow Cook and set the timer for 1 hour.
3. Mix together in a bowl, cornstarch, and water and pour into the pot.
4. Press Sauté. Stir constantly until it thickens. Add the red wine and mix well.
5. Blend the berries that were set aside and add to the thickened berries.
6. Can be served either hot or cold. Serve with milk or cream.

Pumpkin Custard

Servings: 4

Total time taken: 45 minutes + chilling time

Ingredients:

- 1 cup cooked pumpkin, diced
- 3 eggs
- 2 tablespoons full fat coconut milk
- 2 tablespoons maple syrup
- ¼ teaspoon ginger
- 1 teaspoon pumpkin pie spice

Directions:

1. Pour water into the inner pot to cover at least an inch from the bottom.
2. Blend together all the ingredients. Grease ovenproof ramekins and pour the blended mixture into the ramekins. Keep it 2/3 full.
3. Carefully place the ramekins in the inner pot.
4. Lock lid and select Multi-grain and default time to 40 minutes.
5. Let the pressure release naturally for 15 minutes then serve.

Spiced Apple Crunch

Servings: 8-10

Total time taken: 30 min

Ingredients:

- 6 apples, cored, sliced
- 2 cups dry bread crumbs
- ½ cup butter, melted
- Zest of 2 lemons
- Juice of 2 lemons
- 1 teaspoon ground cinnamon
- 1/8 teaspoon ground nutmeg
- ½ cup sugar
- 2 cups water

Directions:

1. Grease a baking dish with butter. Mix together in a bowl, breadcrumbs, sugar, cinnamon, lemon juice and zest.
2. Place a single layer of apples in the dish. Sprinkle some of the mixture over it. Repeat this step until all the apples and the mixture is used up.
3. Drizzle butter all over. Cover with foil.
4. Pour water into inner pot and place trivet in it. Place the dish over trivet.
5. Lock lid and press Steam and set time to 15 minutes. Once time is up do natural release and serve warm.

French Orange Crème

Servings: 12

Total time taken: 20 minutes + chilling

Ingredients:

- 9 yolks
- 1 ½ cups milk
- 1 cup sugar
- 1 ½ cups cream
- 1 teaspoon orange zest
- Blackberries to garnish
- Blackberry syrup to top

Directions:

1. Pour milk and cream into a saucepan and place it over medium heat. Remove from heat when it just begins to bubble and cool. Whisk together yolks and sugar until sugar dissolves.
2. Add orange zest. Pour milk mixture into this and whisk until well combined.
3. Pour into ramekins and cover each ramekin with foil. Pour 1½ cups water into the inner pot. Place steamer rack in it. Place the ramekins over it. Lock lid and press Steam and set time to 10 minutes.
4. Perform a quick release then remove ramekins. Uncover, cool and chill. Garnish blackberries and blackberry syrup over it and serve.

Crème Brule

Servings: 6 -8

Total time taken: 15 min

Ingredients:

- 6 egg yolks
- ¼ cup granulated sugar
- 1 teaspoon vanilla extract
- ¼ cup granulated sugar
- 4 tablespoons very fine sugar
- 1 ½ cups heavy cream

Directions:

1. Whisk together in a bowl, yolks, sugar, and salt. Add cream and vanilla and whisk until well blended.
2. Strain the entire mixture into a pitcher. Pour this mixture into 4 - 5 custard cups or ramekins. Cover each of the cups with aluminum foil.
3. Place a trivet at the bottom of the inner pot. Pour about 1-½ cups of water. Place the cups on the trivet. Lock lid and cook on High for 6 minutes. Let the pressure release naturally.
4. Remove the cups after a while. Uncover and cool.
5. Serve warm or chilled. Serve sprinkled with fine sugar.

Caramel Custard

Servings: 6
Total time taken: 45 min + chilling time.

Ingredients:

- 2 cups milk
- 4 eggs, beaten
- ½ cup + 8 tablespoons white sugar
- 2 tablespoons water
- 2 tablespoons hot water or as required
- 1 teaspoon vanilla extract

Directions:

1. Place a heavy saucepan over medium heat. Add ½cup sugar and 2 tablespoons water and heat until it begins to boil. Lower heat slightly and cook without stirring until golden brown syrup is formed.
2. Remove from heat and let it cool for a minute. Add hot water and stir. Pour into a baking dish or divide and pour a little into each ramekin or custard cups. Let it cool. It will harden.
3. Meanwhile, place a saucepan over low heat. Add 8tablespoons sugar and milk. Stir constantly until sugar is dissolved and milk is lukewarm. Remove from heat and add eggs and vanilla extract. Whisk well. Pour the egg mixture over the caramel set dish or ramekins.
4. Place a trivet inside the inner pot. Pour 2 cups of water. Place the dish over the trivet.
5. Lock lid select Multi Grain and set time for 15 minutes. Allow 15 minutes for a natural release then chill. To serve, run a knife all around the edges of the pan and invert on to a plate. Sprinkle nutmeg and confectioners' sugar and serve.

Stuffed Peaches

Servings: 10

Total time taken: 20 min + chilling time

Ingredients:

- 10 peaches
- 4 tablespoons butter, melted
- ½ cup maple sugar
- ½ cup flour
- 2 tablespoons almonds, finely chopped
- 1 teaspoon ground cinnamon
- 1 teaspoon almond extract
- 2 cups water

Directions:

1. Slice the top of the peach and discard it. Carefully remove the pits using a knife
2. Mix together butter, flour, cinnamon, ½ teaspoon almond extract. Stuff this mixture into each peach.
3. Pour water and ½ teaspoon almond extract into the Pressure Ccoker. Place a trivet. Place peaches in a heatproof bowl over the trivet.
4. Lock lid and select Steam and cook time to 3 minutes. Quick release the pressure. Cool ard serve with vanilla ice cream.

Apricot Crisp

Servings: 6

Total time taken: 2 hrs. 10 min

Ingredients:

- 1 can (20 ounces) apricots, drained, sliced
- ½ cup packed light brown sugar
- 1/3 cup ground crackers
- 2 tablespoons butter, unsalted, divided

Directions:

1. Grease the inside of the inner pot with cooking spray.
2. Layer with half the apricot slices followed by half the cracker crumbs followed by brown sugar and finally half the butter. Repeat the above layer.
3. Close the lid. Select the Slow Cook function and set the timer for 2 hours. Serve warm.

FRUIT	ELECTRIC PRESSURE COOKER (10-12PSI)	STOVETOP PRESSURE COOKER (13-15PSI)	PRESSURE SELECTION	OPENING METHOD
Apples	3	2	High	Natural
Apricot (fresh)	4	2	High	Natural
Apricot (dried)	4	4	High	Natural
Blackberries	8	8	High	Natural
Blueberries	6	6	High	Natural
Cherries	2	2	High	Natural
Mango	7	5	High	Natural
Orange, wedges	15	10	High	Natural

Berry Compote

Servings: 12

Total time taken: 20 min

Ingredients:

- 2 cups blueberries, divided
- 2 cups blackberries, sliced
- 2 cups raspberries
- 4 tablespoons lemon juice
- 2 tablespoons water mixed with 2 tablespoons cornstarch
- 1 ½ cups sugar

Directions:

1. Add raspberries, blackberries, sugar, and lemon juice and 1/3 of the blueberries into the inner pot. Stir.
2. Lock lid and press Steam and timer to 3 minutes. Release excess pressure after 10 minutes. Select the Sauté function. Add cornstarch mixture and stir constantly until the mixture thickens.
3. Add remaining blueberries and stir. Chill and serve.

Caramel Fondue

Servings: 6

Total time taken: 20 min

Ingredients:

- 12 soft caramels, unwrapped
- 3 tablespoons mini marshmallows
- 3 tablespoons heavy cream or milk
- ¼ teaspoon fine sea salt

Directions:

1. Add caramels, milk, salt, and mini marshmallows to the inner pot.
2. Close the lid. Select the Manual option and set the timer for 20 minutes.
3. Perform a quick release then serve with fruits or cookies or pretzels.

FRUIT	ELECTRIC PRESSURE COOKER (10-12PSI)	STOVETOP PRESSURE COOKER (13-15PSI)	PRESSURE SELECTION	OPENING METHOD
Apples	3	2	High	Natural
Apricot (fresh)	4	2	High	Natural
Apricot (dried)	4	4	High	Natural
Blackberries	8	8	High	Natural
Blueberries	6	6	High	Natural
Cherries	2	2	High	Natural
Mango	7	5	High	Natural
Orange, wedges	15	10	High	Natural

Pressure Cooker Measurements Charts and Guidelines

The Pasta Measurements are For servings of 2 people

LONG PASTAS	DRY PASTA Measured with Hand	COOKED PASTA Measured in Cups
Angel Hair	2 to 3inches (circumference)	2 cups
Fettuccine	2 to 3inches (circumference)	2 cups
Linguine	2 to 3inches (circumference)	2 cups
Spaghetti	2 to 3inches (circumference)	2 cups
Thin Spaghetti	2 to 3inches (circumference)	2 cups

SHORT PASTAS	DRY PASTA Measured in Cups
Macaroni Elbows	2 cups
Penne	2 cups
Rigatoni	2 cups
Rotini	2 cups
Farfalle	2 cups
Fusilli	2 cups

Canned Soups and Sauces used in this cookbook

- The sizes used in this recipe is 14 oz. (Equivalent to 1 and ¾ cups)

Frozen Bagged Vegetables used in this cookbook

- The sizes used is 14 oz. this typically feeds about 4 people (or 2 really hungry teenagers)

Optimum Servings for the recipes used in this cookbook

- The ideal portion size in this recipe cookbook is between 4 to 8 servings. The reason behind this is that to get the most use out of your pressure cooker and the recipes is to not over crowd your ingredients.

Pressure Cooker Bone Broth Stocks

The recipes in this collection does require the use of broths and stocks, Follow this recipe to create your own healthy Bone Broths. This is an easy to follow Bone Broth recipe that you can make at home and use it as an alternative to store bought chicken, beef, or pork Bone Broths.

INGREDIENTS

- 2 pounds fresh animal bones (either chicken, beef, pork etc.) You can inquire about fresh bones from your local butcher or grocer.
- 2 purple onion, peeled and cut in half
- 2 large carrots, chopped into chunks
- 2 celery sticks cut in half
- ½ tablespoon sea salt
- 10 cups water

PREPARATION

1. For a clearer broth you will need to blanch the bones first. In a large soup pot, fill it halfway full and let it come to a boil. Once boiling add your bones into the pot and let it cook for about 5 minutes. Then strain and rinse the bones under cold running water for 5 minutes. This will wash away all the impurities of the animal bones.

2. Once done blanching add the bones to a cheesecloth along with your vegetable ingredients. Secure the bone broth bag with twine.

3. Add the water to your pressure cooking pot. Then add in your bone broth bag, sprinkle the sea salt and lock lid. Set to Soup and change the time to 90 minutes. Set timer. Once timer goes off, release pressure naturally. Let broth cool then remove the bone broth bag and bottle up your homemade bone broth in mason jars and keep refrigerated until use. Or you can freeze 2 cup portions of it in freezer containers.

Bone and Vegetable Broths

Broths are one of the most versatile ingredients. While time consuming, a good, homemade, broth is much healthier than the store bought version because you are in control of the ingredients. Almost any dish made with water can be substituted with a broth to bring more complex flavors to your dishes.

This is an easy to follow Bone Broth recipe that you can make at home and use it as an alternative to store bought chicken, beef, or pork Bone Broths Homemade stocks.

Bone Broth

Ingredients:
2 pounds fresh animal bones (either chicken, beef, pork etc.) You can inquire about fresh bones from your local butcher
2 purple onion, peeled and cut in half
2 large carrots, chopped into chunks
2 celery sticks cut in half
1/2 tablespoon sea salt
10 cups water

Instructions:
For a clearer broth you will need to blanch the bones first. In a large soup pot, fill it halfway full and let it come to a boil. Once boiling add your bones into the pot and let it cook for about 5 minutes. Then strain and rinse the bones under cold running water for 5 minutes. This will wash away all the impurities of the animal bones.

Once done blanching add the bones to a cheesecloth along with your vegetable ingredients. Secure the bone broth bag with twine.

Add the water to a large stock pot. Then add in your bone broth bag, sprinkle the sea salt. Simmer stock for 30 minutes uncovered or until the stock has been reduced by about one cup.

Strain and discard ingredients.

Vegetable Broth

Ingredients:
1 tablespoon olive oil
1 large onion
2 stalks celery
2 large carrots
1 bunch leeks
8 cloves garlic, smashed
8 sprigs fresh parsley
6 sprigs fresh thyme
2 bay leaves
1 teaspoon salt
8 cups water

Instructions:
Chop scrubbed vegetables into 1-1 1/2-inch chunks.

In a large stock pot, heat oil. Sauté the onions, carrots, leeks, garlic, parsley, thyme and bay leaves.

Cook over high heat stirring frequently until the onions have turned translucent.

Add salt and water and bring to a boil. Lower heat and simmer, uncovered, for about 30 minutes or until the stock has been reduced by about 1 cup.

Strain and discard vegetables.

Fruits	Fresh, Cooking Time (in Minutes)	Dried, Cooking Time (in Minutes)
Apples, in slices or pieces	2 – 3	3 – 4
Apples, whole	3 – 4	4 – 6
Apricots, whole or halves	2 – 3	3 – 4
Peaches	2 – 3	4 – 5
Pears, whole	3 – 4	4 – 6
Pears, slices or halves	2 – 3	4 – 5
Prunes	2 – 3	4 – 5
Raisins	N/A	4 – 5

Rice & Grain	Water Quantity (Grain : Water ratios)	Cooking Time (in Minutes)
Barley, pearl	1:4	25 – 30
Barley, pot	1:3 ~ 1:4	25 – 30
Congee, thick	1:4 ~ 1:5	15 – 20
Congee, thin	1:6 ~ 1:7	15 – 20
Couscous	1:2	5 – 8
Corn, dried, half	1:3	25 – 30
Kamut, whole	1:3	10 – 12
Millet	1:1 2/3	10 – 12

Your Spice Rack

Coriander
Dried coriander seeds are a staple in South East Asian cooking and is found in garam masala and other Indian curries. The fresh coriander leaves are used mostly as a garnish or added to broths to give it a more citrus note.

Curcuma/Turmeric
Also known as turmeric and is found in a lot of South East Asian cuisines such as Thai curries and dishes.

Cinnamon
Mostly used in baking and in coffees and teas, it's a wonderful spice to add aroma to your stews and desserts.

Oregano
Oregano is a common herb in Italian cuisines and go great in pizza sauce and grilled vegetables, meat and fish.

Saffron
Saffron has a delicious honey and grassy notes to it and is a beloved spice of Asian and Middle Eastern cuisines. It's commonly used in baking and flavoring rice and pastas.

Bay Leaf
This aromatic spice goes great in meat sauces, and thick pasta sauces. It's also a favorite in hearty stews and stocks.

Dried/Fresh Garlic
Aromatic and delicious in just about anything. Dried garlic is very easy to use to season and marinate meats, fish and vegetables.

Paprika
Favorite spice used to season rice, stews and sausages.

Black Pepper
Popular spice used to season foods and is a staple in every kitchen.

Sea Salt
Used in roasting and as a brine for a variety of meats and seafood.

Cumin
Mainly used for highly spiced foods and is a popular spice in Indian, and Mexican cooking. It goes great with stews and grilled meats, especially lamb and chicken dishes.

Clove
Used in Asian and Middle Eastern cuisines in curries and marinades.

Mediterranean Spice Mix

- 2 tablespoons dried cumin
- 2 tablespoons ground coriander
- 1 tablespoon dried oregano
- 3 tablespoons dried rosemary
- 2 teaspoons ground cinnamon
- 1/2 teaspoon sea salt

Mix all ingredients in a bowl and store in an air-tight container for up to two months.

Bread Knife

Carving Knife

Cleaver

Santoku Knife

Chef Knife

Boning Knife

Utility Knife

Filleting Knife

Small Pairing Knife

Year Round Vegetables

January - December

Amaranth

Arrowroot

Banana Squash

Bell Peppers

Black Eyed Peas

Black Radish

Bok Choy

Burdock Root

Cabbage

Carrots

Celeriac (Celery Root)

Celery

Cherry Tomatoes

Chinese Eggplants

Galangal Root

Leek

Lettuce

Mushrooms

Olives

Onions

Parsnips

Pearl Onions

Potatoes

Rutabagas

Salad Savoy

Vegetables in Spring

March - April - May

Artichokes

Asparagus

Broccoli

Butter Lettuce

Cactus

Chayote Squash

Chives

Collard Greens

Corn

Fava Beans

Fennel

Fiddlehead Ferns

Green Beans

Morel Mushrooms

Mustard Greens

Pea Pods

Peas

Purple Asparagus

Radicchio

Ramps

Red Leaf Lettuce

Rhubarb

Snow Peas

Sorrel

Spinach

Spring Baby Lettuce

Vegetables in Fall

September – October - November

Acorn Squash

Belgian Endive

Black Salsify

Broccoli

Brussels Sprouts

Butter Lettuce

Buttercup Squash

Butternut Squash

Cauliflower

Chayote Squash

Chinese Long Beans

Delicata Squash

Diakon Radish

Endive

Garlic

Ginger

Jalapeno Peppers

Jerusalem Artichoke

Kohlrabi

Pumpkin

Radicchio

Sweet Dumpling Squash

Sweet Potatoes

Swiss Chard

Turnips

Winter Squash

Vegetables in Winter

December - January - February

Belgian Endive

Brussels Sprouts

Buttercup Squash

Collard Greens

Delicata Squash

Kale

Leeks

Sweet Dumpling Squash

Sweet Potatoes

Turnips

Winter Squash

Vegetables in Summer

June - July - August

Beets

Bell Peppers

Butter Lettuce

Chayote Squash

Chinese Long Beans

Corn

Crookneck Squash

Cucumbers

Eggplant

Endive

Garlic

Green Beans

Green Soybeans (Edamame)

Jalapeno Peppers

Lima Beans

Manoa Lettuce

Okra

Peas

Radishes

Shallots

Sugar Snap Peas

Summer Squash

Tomatillo

Tomatoes

Winged Beans

Yukon Gold Potatoes

PRESSURE COOKER ACCESSORES

1. Extra Silicone Sealing Rings

- **Silicone Sealing Ring** – Pressure Cooker Sealing Rings' life expectancy varies. If steam starts to leak around the lid, replace the Pressure Cooker Sealing Ring immediately.
- **Genuine Sweet & Savory Edition Silicone Sealing Ring – Two Pack** – Since the sealing ring will absorb the smell of the food in the pot, many users also like to use separate sealing rings for cooking savory dishes and desserts.

2. Steamer Racks

- **Stainless Steel Steaming Rack Stand 5" Diameter** – this is the most commonly used accessory for cooking in Pressure Cooker. *A must for using the Pot-In-Pot method!*
- **Stainless Steel Steamer Basket** – Another steamer basket we use frequently (i.e. ribs!)

3. Containers

Any oven-safe containers will be safe to use in the Pressure Cooker (i.e. Stainless Steel, Silicone, Corelle bowls)

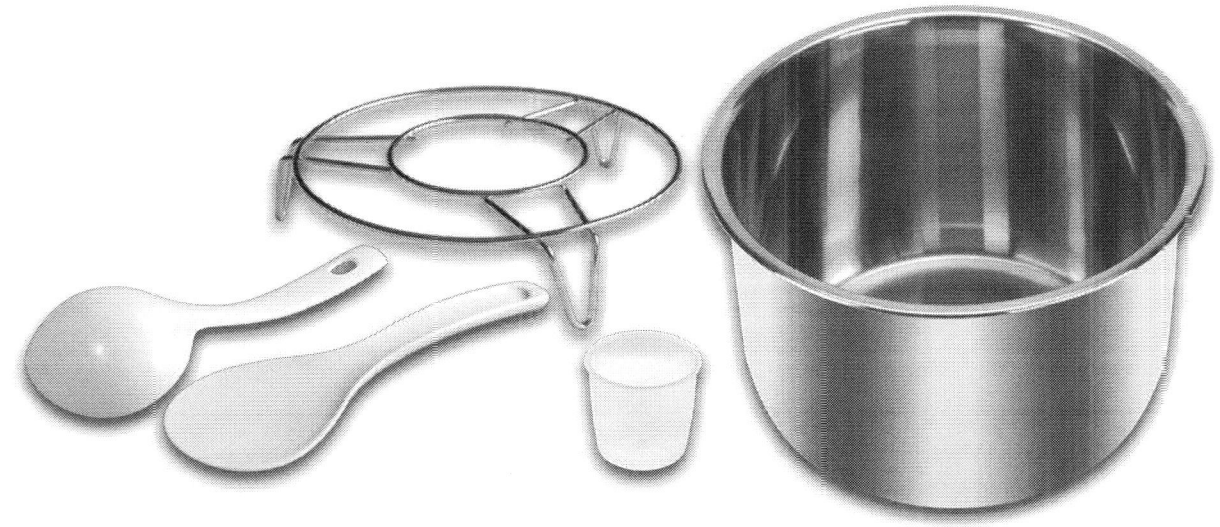

Thank You

One of the many advantages of cooking in a Pressure Cooker is that you will be able to cook food in batches and freeze it up for future use. This not only saves time but effort as well. You will be able to cook delicious and nutritious food by making use of the recipes that have been provided in this book. You will simply need to plan ahead and make sure that your pantry is well stocked.

The next time you have your friends or family over for a meal, you can whip up a delicious three-course meal by making use of the recipes given in this book and put your Pressure Cooker to good use. Make use of the various preset modes and different methods of cooking for making a tasty meal.

Made in the USA
San Bernardino, CA
25 October 2017